OH . . . I AM A LIVERPUDLIAN
AND I COME FROM THE
SPION
KOP

SPORT MEDIA
Trinity Mirror North West

Published in Great Britain in 2004 by:
Trinity Mirror Sport Media.
PO Box 48, Old Hall Street,
Liverpool L69 3EB

Executive Editor: Ken Rogers
Production Editor: Paul Dove
Publishing Executive: Dan Willoughby
Art Editor: Rick Cooke

ISBN 0-9546871-1-6

Printed and bound by Scotprint, Haddington, Scotland

Contents

*'The fans here are the greatest in the land.
They know the game and they know what they
want to see. The people on the Kop make you feel
great – yet humble. I'm just one of the people who
stands on the Kop. They think the same as I do, and
I think the same as they do. It's a kind of marriage
of people who like each other.'*

Bill Shankly

*'It was Bill's life.
Liverpool Football Club and the Kop, that is. Bill
felt close to the Kop from the start.
It was the instant humour and the singing of the
songs all together that appealed to him. I only went
to a few matches at that time but I knew how close
Bill was to the Kop. He would have been very, very
sad to see it go but it is progress. Out of the ashes
will come a great new stadium. I've never been on
the Kop but I'm a Kopite'*

Nessie Shankly

POOR SCOUSER TOMMY

Let me tell you the story of a poor boy,
Who was sent far away from his home,
To fight for his king and his country,
And also the old folks back home.

So they put him in a Highland division,
Sent him off to a far foreign land,
Where the flies swarm around in their thousands,
And there's nothing to see but the sand.

Now the battle it started next morning,
Under the Arabian sun,
I remember that poor Scouser Tommy,
He was shot by an old Nazi gun.

As he lay on the battlefield dying, dying, dying,
With the blood gushing out of his head, of his head,
As he lay on the battlefield dying, dying, dying,
These were the last words he said.

Oh I am a Liverpudlian and I come from the Spion Kop,
I like to sing, I like to shout,
I get thrown out quite a lot (every week!)
I support a team that's dressed in red,
It's a team that you all know.
It's a team that we call LIVERPOOL,
To glory we will go.
We've won the league, we've won the cup,
And we've been to Europe too.
We played the Toffees for a laugh and we left 'em feeling blue, 5-0.
One, two, one two three, one two three four, FIVE NIL!
Rush scored one, Rush scored two, Rush scored three and Rush scored
four, nah nah nah nah nah nah nah nah nah . . .

The first four verses are to the tune of 'The Red River Valley'. The rest is to the tune of 'The Sash'. Poor Scouser Tommy was originally penned in the 1960s and the popular version now has some subtle changes from the original. The line 'under the Arabian sun' was originally 'under the Libyan sun' and you'll hear Kopites standing side by side singing both versions, depending on which era they're from. The original didn't contain the 'I' in 'And I come from the Spion Kop', either. It was originally just 'And come from the Spion Kop'. The 'I get thrown out quite a lot' is often sung as 'I go there quite a lot' and there are various other words that have been exchanged for similar ones over time. And of course, the 'Rush scored one, Rush scored two, Rush scored three and Rush scored four' bit only appeared after a certain Merseyside derby at Goodison Park in 1982.

Let me tell you the story

S pion Kop.
It's arguably the most famous suburb in Liverpool.

Never mind Edge Hill, Kensington, West Derby, Toxteth, Huyton, Walton, Aigburth, Anfield or anywhere else.

If you asked a Liverpudlian where he came from in the '60s, '70s or '80s then he'd tell you 'Spion Kop'.

Mind you, when you've got a messiah leading the club like Bill Shankly who once filled a form in and put his address down as 'Anfield' then it's no wonder that followers of Liverpool Football Club had an affinity with the Kop.

And that's what this book is all about - Kopites. The group of people who turned what was once just a pile of cinder into the most famous, most feared, most respected and most ▶

▶ celebrated terracing in world football.

Man United had the Stretford End. Arsenal the North Bank. You'd find Evertonians on the Gwladys Street and Geordies in the Gallowgate End.

Famous? In their own rights. But not a patch on the Spion Kop.

Anfield has never needed a cheesy or tacky label like 'Theatre of Dreams' to sell itself.

It had the Kop. With dreams and songs to sing.

Even now, in the era of all-seater stadia, The Kop remains the most famous stand in any English football ground.

Liverpool and the Kop go hand in hand.

To the tabloid headline writers, the Kop IS Liverpool. How many other clubs do you see regularly referred to in the press by the name on one of their stands? None.

That's the impact, the lasting effect on the minds of those not associated with Liverpool, that the Kop has had. Anyone who stood on it will tell you that's not surprising.

The Kop was more than concrete and steel. More than an imposing structure that dominated the Anfield skyline. It was a church. A community centre. A way of life. All rolled into one.

Kopites didn't just attend Anfield for the football, they came for everything else that went with it too. They came, in droves, to stand on the Spion Kop. Their Kop. The laughs, the banter, the spirit. The status of being a Kopite.

Singing, shouting, chanting, celebrating, cat-calling, taking the p*** or - if you had a copy of the Echo handy - taking a p*** down the back of the fella in front of you. Those 25,000 Reds stood shoulder to shoulder, breathing down the visiting goalkeeper's neck.

Visiting goalies didn't just have what Liverpool put in front of them to contend with. They had an entire stand trying to suck the ball into the net behind them. They were intimidating without being nasty. They didn't need to be.

The noise and size of the support was enough in itself to have grown men trembling in their boots.

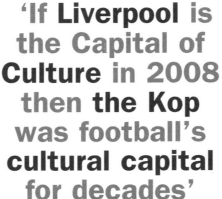

'If **Liverpool is the Capital of Culture in 2008** then **the Kop was football's cultural capital for decades**'

Standing on the Kop wasn't a place to be for the faint-hearted either.

One current banner seen around the fields of Anfield Road in recent times says simply: 'Above Us, Only Sky'. The quote, from a John Lennon classic, didn't apply to the Kop. As well as the impressive and imposing steel roof, plumes of cigarette smoke would drift upwards into the air.

On some nights you could see steam rising off the Kop, like there was a cauldron on the boil behind the goal. Things would reach boiling point when Liverpool scored.

A crescendo of noise erupted as the Kop surged forward. It was bedlam. You'd find yourself carried forward and not be able to do anything about it.

Then, when the surge relented, you'd be carried back to somewhere near to where you started. Finding your favourite spec on the Kop was one thing, staying in it for the full 90 minutes was another.

If Liverpool is the Capital of Culture in 2008 then the Kop was football's cultural capital for decades. It led the way in terms of noise, singing, colour, humour, chanting, ingenuity and even fashion. The rest have been playing catch-up ever since.

Ten years ago, the old Spion Kop was demolished to make way for a new all-seater stand. A decade on, this book looks back on the days of the old Kop - and how it is now. Don't be expecting a chronological crawl through history, though.

When you stood on the Kop watching the mighty Reds you were never quite sure where you'd be carried to next and this book aims to reflect that. Expect the unexpected.

The highs, the lows. The heroes, the villains. The pain and the glory. You'll find it all here.

A unique crowd with a unique history deserves to have its story told and who better to tell the story than those who stood on, played in front of and even came up against the Kop?

'Oh . . . I Am A Liverpudlian And I Come From The Spion Kop' tells you the story of those who support a team that's dressed in red, a team that you all know.

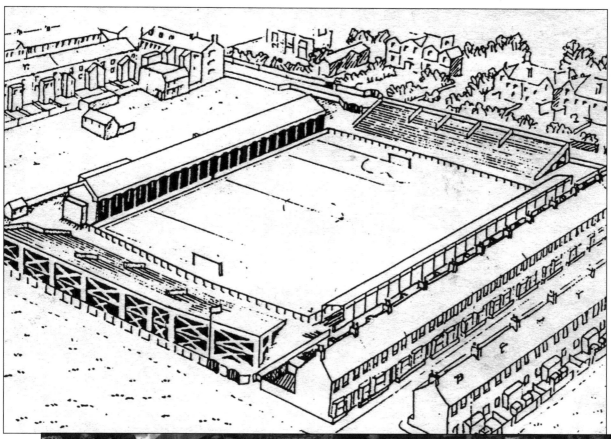

From this to this: A drawing of Anfield in 1894-95 with uncovered terracing behind either goal. The Kop is on the left and the Kemlyn Road terraced properties to its right which were demolished as the club developed the Centenary Stand. Above: the Kop in full song in 1992

Let's hear it for the boys in Red: Brian Hall celebrates a goal, along with Kevin Keegan – and 20,000 delirious Kopites

Off to a far foreign land

Defeat isn't a word that was particularly associated with the Spion Kop. However, it was defeat for a group of Liverpudlian soldiers that played a significant part in giving the famous old terrace its name.

In January 1900, scores of Scousers were part of the Lancashire Fusiliers that went to battle in the Boer War.

A fierce battle took place on a hill near Ladysmith, South Africa, that was known locally as Spioenkop Hill. The battle ended in defeat with more than 300 of the Lancashire Fusiliers losing their lives.

Six years later and that South African hill would become part of Merseyside folklore forever. The Kop itself was built as a reward for Liverpool supporters after the club lifted its second league championship in 1906. Anfield already had a small terraced area at the Walton Breck Road end but chairman John Houlding and club secretary 'Honest' John McKenna decided there was room for improvement.

A steep, cinder bank with wooden steps and no roof was designed by well-respected architect Archibald Leitch and constructed that summer. All they needed now was a name. At first they were, like a batsman out of his crease, well and truly stumped.

'Walton Breck Bank' sounded like something where you kept your shillings while they'd have never fitted 'The Walton Breck Road end' on match tickets.

The season kicked off and the new stand, which held around 20,000 spectators and gave some splendid views across Stanley Park, remained nameless.

It was Ernest Edwards, sports editor of the Liverpool Echo at the time, who had a moment of inspiration during that campaign.

Edwards said that Liverpool's new terracing reminded him of the hill where the battle of Ladysmith had taken place; so why not call the stand the Spion Kop?

There could have been a very different response if the battle had taken place on Mount Kilimanjaro but, as it was, the name stuck.

However, Liverpool's wasn't the first Kop. ▶

'Six years later and that **South African hill** would become part of **Merseyside folklore** forever'

The same title had previously been given to terracing at Woolwich Arsenal but the name never caught on. The singing still hasn't at Highbury.

Arsenal's old North Bank gives you an idea of what could have been for Anfield if it wasn't for Edwards.

His suggestion was probably greeted with such enthusiasm because local men had lost their lives on Spioenkop Hill.

It was almost as if a belated memorial had been put up in Liverpool and everyone liked it.

A 1-0 win over Stoke on September 1, in blazing hot heat, was watched by 30,000 fans with many becoming the first to ever watch a game from the Kop.

Anfield may have initially been Everton's ground but their supporters never stood on the Kop as we know it.

For the eight years they played at Anfield - between 1884 and 1892 - their supporters had to make do with that unremarkable terracing on Walton Breck Road.

The Kop was entirely a Liverpool institution and the next major change came in 1928, largely thanks to the British weather.

Standing on the Kop with 20,000 other people was one thing. Standing on it in torrential rain, gale force winds or even through thunder and lightning was another.

The roofless Kop was an unpleasant place to be on a dreadful day, even for hardened dockers who'd regularly be battered by the elements down by the Mersey.

The prospect of soggy flat caps and wet ciggies all-round wasn't exactly going to attract people to Anfield, so the board of directors decided the time had come to build a roof.

Mr J Watson Cabre, an architect from Great Crosby, was put in charge of the new development and by the start of the 1928/29 season Anfield had the first roofed-in Kop in the country.

Part of the terracing was also redeveloped during the construction work so apart from the cinder hill beneath the terracing and three concrete staircases, Kopites had virtually a brand new home.

Up to 28,000 fans could now be accommodated,

Flag pole corner: The Kop around 1906 and, above right, the same view in 1958

and the roof - 80 foot high, 425 feet long and 131 feet wide - dominated the Anfield skyline.

The outside walls and six internal stanchions of the Kop were said to carry a massive 45,500 square feet of roof space - into which 91 standard houses could be packed together in one layer.

It was a big roof for a big club who had big ambitions.

As the roof went up so did the entrance price. It now cost one shilling (five pence) to stand on the Kop.

You couldn't afford one of Michael Owen's eyelashes for five pence these days but, nonetheless, that was still a hefty price for the majority to pay, particularly as unemployment was beginning to bite on Merseyside.

The new-look Kop was officially opened by the President of the Football League, and former secretary, director and chairman of the club, John McKenna on August 25.

Liverpool beat Bury 3-0 that day in front of 40,000 fans and McKenna was reportedly presented with a gold cigar to mark the occasion.

Far more significant for the 40,000 who weren't presented with gold cigars was the moment when Billy Millar opened the scoring for Liverpool.

With just 50 seconds on the clock Millar headed home and the new Kop erupted for the first time.

It was like a volcano had gone off. The acoustics were fantastic, the noise was something else.

The Kop had a wall like no other in football - a wall of noise.

Not only had putting a roof over the terracing stopped the rain from getting in, it had stopped the noise from getting out.

Liverpool Football Club had a 12th man.

But it would be another 30 years or so, and the inspiration of one man, before they got the best out of him.

'The Kop had a wall like no other in football – a wall of noise. Liverpool Football Club had a 12th man'

'I can still feel that surge of pride at 10 to 3 as the teams were read out'

In the beginning I was never hard enough for the Kop.

Tales of drunken dockers, big lads who yockered in your hair and robbed your chip money sent me scuttling for the safety of the Anfield Road end.

But it wasn't safe at all.

This was the late Sixties when no segregation meant nutters in Bakers, braces and boots flew past you knocking lumps out of shaven heads, while you soldered your hands to the crash barrier for fear of losing your life or, even worse, your spec.

They were the Alun Evans' seasons. Silver-less years but golden days. Away from home Liverpool were Stoke City but at Anfield they were Real Madrid.

The players steamrollered opponents into submission, the manager's charisma set him apart from other mortals and the Kop was the greatest collective mass of passion, wit and song in any walk of British life.

I can still feel the surge of pride at 10 to three as the teams were read out. The Wrigleys moving faster. The churn in the pit of the stomach, small at first, then spreading.

The sudden rush of adrenalin in the split second between Liverpool's substitute being announced and Gerry Marsden uttering "Whey-en," – the signal for that massive red and white shutter to rise and block everything else out on the horizon.

The faces on the away fans struck dumb by a vision, like George Best worth the admission fee alone, some of them raising kids above their shoulders to glimpse the eighth wonder of the world.

The men in the stands, standing. Faces riveted to the Kop. Watching grace being sung before the meal.

There were few banners then: Europe had yet to be conquered. No adidas shirts or multi-coloured scarves. Money had yet to conquer. Just a wall of sound and a crashing sea of red and white.

I plunged into it on November 21, 1970. It was derby day, my second day as a teenager, and possibly the most delirious day of my life. Everton were champions and playing like it.

The Horse (Joe Royle) and the Rat (Alan Whittle) had put them two up with 20 minutes to go.

Misery stared me in the face as well as a surrounding knot of Evertonians on the outer edges of the Kop. (I never dared stand in the middle then. They were feudal plots handed down by fathers).

When Heighway scored, a huge wave that turned into a Blackpool rollercoaster lifted me and nearly unhinged my neck from my spine.

When Toshack scored I flew a full 30 feet down the terrace and was thrown back like whiplash.

When Lawler scored the winner I went under like a dog tied to an old bed.

I was sucked up, heaved back about 15 feet, tossed into the air and landed lodged between two men trying to make love.

For the remaining six minutes my feet didn't touch the deck and when they did I was minus one patent leather Chelsea boot and bus fare.

I walked home to Huyton, a grin splitting my face and the concrete splitting my sole. It was the most lethal Ecstasy a teenager could taste.

In those days the Kop starred in its own movies and the players vied for best supporting actor.

The film and sound crews turned up to record not a footballing phenomenon but a social one.

Rock groups like Pink Floyd put us on best ▶

Home and away: Two evocative pictures of Liverpool fans on Mersey derby day. Right: Getting in the mood at Anfield in 1972 and, below, making their presence felt at Goodison in the same year

Derby delirium: A memorable day on the Kop as Chris Lawler is mobbed following his winning goal in November, 1970 which capped a remarkable 3-2 comeback

▶ selling albums. Kop albums were recorded.

Foreign documentary teams sent their Dimblebys to record all this happening.

As the '70s turned into '80s and Liverpool went for world domination the players became stars.

They less and less needed a goal sucking in.

There were the breathless nights of emotion like St Etienne, but the Beatle-wigged Kopite had become Scouser Tommy, sent far away from his home to Paris, London and Rome.

That's where the big nights were. Domestic success had become like a rates bill – an annual demand paid in sobering instalments.

As the '90s approached, the Kop had changed.

Reduced capacity, success over-kill and increased traffic from York and Yeovil transforming its nature.

I headed for the stands when a mate moaned his wallet had grown but his body hadn't, but the eyes and the spirit were still there on big occasions.

The Kop really belonged to the '60s, '70s and part of the '80s when the mound was packed and you swayed with reckless abandon on a wild trip minus seatbelts or brakes.

We, more than any other set of fans, should appreciate why, sadly, the joyriding had to stop.

The Kopite wasn't wittier than the man on the Gwladys Street. He wasn't a better singer than a Stretford Ender.

But he was part of a collective voice, generosity, attitude, tradition and spirit that was unique.

'The Kop really **belonged** to the '60s, '70s and part of the '80s when the mound was **packed** and you swayed with **reckless abandon** on a wild trip minus **seatbelts**'

My first experience of the Kop was in May 1970. I was still a student at Warwick University but had decided to sign professional for Liverpool on completing my degree in June.

As a student I was quite surprised to be called by Mr Bill Shankly who invited me to play in Gerry Byrne's testimonial for a Celebrity XI against a Liverpool side.

Not only was it my first visit to Anfield but at 22 it was my first ever visit to Liverpool itself. It was a filthy night with rain and sleet, but I recall that 50,000 people were there.

The two teams walked side by side to the centre of the pitch and I stood next to an Everton full-back who was playing in the Celebrity team.

With total honesty and complete naivety I quietly said to him: "Which end is the Kop?".

He looked at me as if I had come from another planet and pointed to the bulging end rather than just the full end.

That was my first experience and, of course, there were many more opportunities to play in front of what was very obviously the fanatical end.

I had good games and bad games through my 11 years but I feel extremely fortunate that at no time did I ever feel any animosity from the Kop.

I would have found that very difficult to live with and I am eternally grateful that the Kop always seemed to recognise that I was doing my best.

STEVIE HEIGHWAY

Bowing out: Ronnie Moran helps the injured Steve Heighway off the Anfield pitch as the Kop looks on

Match duty: Two Bobbies are called into action as a packed Kop awaits the heroes in red in the '60s

Behind the scenes: Bobby Robson with former Liverpool coach and manager Joe Fagan inside Anfield in 1984

'I remember the old Kop, which went back bloody miles!'

I loved Liverpool. I just thought it was a great cathedral and a great place to play. I remember the old Kop, which went back bloody miles. I don't know how many it held – maybe 18-20,000 – everybody standing.

Those are the days that I remember; the swell of the Kop, the surge of the Kop, the singing of the Kop. Oh, it was a great place. I enjoyed going to Liverpool when I was with Ipswich. I never won. I remember getting a 3-3 draw one day. They were great days.

It always seems to be a cauldron there. The roar of the Kop; the enthusiasm within the public. It spills on to the pitch, I think.

There was always a smell of adrenalin at Liverpool, I tell you. I just think it's been one of the great stadiums of all time, for years and years and years. You have produced, over the years, fantastic teams.

SIR BOBBY ROBSON

Kop support was above anything else and straight from the heart. Those supporters lifted players to undreamed of heights.

I have two personal memories from standing on the Kop as a lad before the war.

Sunderland, in the days of Bobby Gurney and Raich Carter, were the smartest turned out team I had ever seen. And I remember cracking my head on a barrier and seeing stars of a different kind!

JOE FAGAN

Pick that one out: A perfect view of a Billy Liddell header finding the net in 1952 (top) and Joe Fagan signs in as boss in 1983

A sea of faces:
The happiness
and unique
bond among
Kopites is
there for all to
see as the Kop
smiles for the
camera in the
mid-1950s

'That goal had everyone up on their feet. The place shook. It moved'

The most magical night for me in front of the Kop was St Etienne and I'm sure it was for a lot of people.

We were 2-1 up and needed to score another goal and it didn't look like it was going to happen.

David Fairclough came on and, as everyone knows, he scored the goal that sent us through.

I've watched the game since on video and the last eight minutes or so were hell.

I didn't realise just what a good team they were until I watched it again. That goal just had everybody up on their feet. The place shook. It moved.

It was the one occasion of the 650 games that I played for Liverpool when I was aware of the people in the stands. It was rocking.

They were so anxious that St Etienne may score again and go through and for those last eight minutes it felt like the whole ground was moving. It made me nervous because I was aware of the crowd when, for every other game, I wasn't.

I was normally focused on the game. Occasionally I might hear a comment if I was taking a throw-in on the touchline or something but that night I was aware that everybody was anxious. I loved the night games at Anfield in the cool of the evening.

With the steam coming off the Kop and the steam coming off my red jersey, we were together.

They nicknamed me 'Zico' one year. I was in the twilight of my career and I scored 11 goals. I think five of them were from outfield play and mostly scored at the Kop end. I was letting them fly left foot, right foot and amazingly, considering I was the number two, they nicknamed me Zico. I will always, always have that as my fondest memory.

To be given the name Zico, after that famous Brazilian, I must have been playing as a man possessed. I didn't want it to end. That was probably the most affection they gave me.

I used to be Liverpool's penalty taker and took quite a few in front of the Kop. It was usually fine. Nine out of 10 went in and I just concentrated on striking the ball. I hated to miss them and I remember missing one on my birthday in the FA Cup. That disappointed me more than anything else at the Kop end. It was Bob Paisley's last season, I think, and that miss led us to an exit in the FA Cup. That hurt me. I was very disappointed.

The Kop were great with me, though. They lifted me again and I look at it as a blip on the landscape. I carried on taking penalties after that and carried on knocking them in. They encouraged me and that helped a lot. There were some humorous nights that I remember well too.

We played Grimsby in the cup and were winning quite comfortably. The Kop decided to have some fun and with Grimsby being a fishing town they started to rename us with fish related names. They were singing 'Jimmy Plaice' at Jimmy Case, 'Phil Eel' at me, 'Kenny Dogfish' at Kenny Dalglish and one or two others. It was fantastic. The humour was wonderful.

I wondered how they did it and how it could ring throughout that fantastic mass so quickly. The Kop had great tradition. I remember watching it on television before I even joined Liverpool and saw that somebody had fainted. They were passed down to the bottom over the top of the heads. I'd never seen that before.

I think it was a very happy, warm place,

Supersub to the rescue: David Fairclough scores one of the most famous goals in Kop history, in the 3-1 defeat of St Etienne in 1977

Ray of light: Ray Kennedy finds the target to give the Reds hope of a dramatic European comeback

▶ particularly on a chilly night.

I remember once in the Super Cup and the Kop couldn't see Emlyn Hughes score a goal down at the Anfield Road end.

They chanted 'who scored the goal? who scored the goal?' and the Anfield Road end chanted back that it was Emlyn.

They used to suck the ball in and it was worth a goal or two to attack that end and bomb into it.

When we won the toss and kicked that way, second half we would bombard people.

It was a unique place to play in front of, for me.

I certainly learnt from the Scousers playing alongside me that it was a special place.

It reminded me of when I went to the Nou Camp for the first time and on the way to the pitch there is a chapel. The Kop was my chapel, really, and the defining part of the ground.

Anyone else who played there in a red shirt would probably say that too.

There's one thing I do rue about the Kop – never to have stood there and watched a game.

I've got a lad and it's something I should have done. But that's the way of the world and I've got some great memories of playing in front of it.

'It **reminded me** of when I went to the **Nou Camp** where there is a chapel. The Kop was **my chapel** and the defining part of the **ground**'

Zico's spot of class: A common sight from the Kop was a coolly converted Phil Neal penalty. Above right: David Fairclough celebrates after scoring THAT goal

This one's for you: Kevin Keegan throws the ball into the Kop after Steve Heighway's winner against Leeds in 1974

'Come on. Let's have a go!'

I did it on my home debut against West Ham when I ran out in front of the Kop for the first time. I heard them chanting my name so I put my fist up and it was something they could identify with because I had come off the Kop. Whenever the crowd chanted my name I felt like I was representing them so I acknowledged them with the clenched fist – 'come on, let's have a go'. It was never to cause trouble.

Passion play: The massed ranks of the Kop provide the backdrop for this Joey Jones' effort on goal in 1977

27

'Amazing day they found

There was a feeling that the atmosphere on the Kop was going down the pan somewhat in the 1980s.

Complacency from success, smaller attendances, largely because of unemployment, and the effects of the Heysel disaster all contributed to making the famous terrace quieter than it was in the halcyon days of the '60s and '70s.

What nobody realised though was that in 1987 part of the Kop was to go down the pan. Quite literally.

The builders were in during pre-season to strengthen the crush barriers on the Kop.

They ended up on overtime when a giant hole, 20ft by 15ft, appeared on the terracing.

The work on the crush barriers caused a Victorian sewer, built in the 1860s, under the terracing to

collapse, which in turn caused a shaft leading up to a manhole cover on the Kop to come crashing down with it.

Such was the scale of the repair job that Liverpool were forced to play their first three games of the season away from Anfield while the work was completed rather than play in front of a reduced capacity of what would have been around 22,000.

It was worth the wait. Kenny Dalglish's new-look Liverpool side, featuring John Barnes and Peter Beardsley, finally played in front of the Kop on September 12 and won 2-0.

They didn't lose a single home league game all season, winning 15 of their 20 matches and scoring 49 goals in the process on the way to the title.

Proof positive that while the Kop may have gone down the pan in 1987, the Liverpool team certainly hadn't.

a **tunnel** under the **Kop'**

Going underground: Workmen investigate the Victorian culvert discovered running underneath the Kop in 1987. Work on the terrace (above left) meant postponing the start of the 1987/88 season

Man of the
people:
A fan with
Bill Shankly
at Anfield
before his
testimonial
in 1975

Right:
Another
Anfield
legend, Bob
Paisley in
action during
the 1950s
with the Kop
pictured in
the distant
background

'The atmosphere changed when Shanks came. He was one of us'

I first went on the Kop when it opened. It was just a bank then with no roof on. I lived in Everton Valley back then and it was only a short walk to the ground. My uncle Bill would take me. He'd carry me on his shoulders.

He took me into the ground, on to the Kop, and he put me on the barrier. He'd say "This is where you belong, son" and I'd say "Yes, Uncle Bill."

I didn't realise that would be the start of all the wonderful years that I would be involved with the club because I ended up doing some scouting for them.

I worked for a building firm in Northwich and the foreman, a very hard man, very stout, bowler hat, says to me: "I believe you have something to do with Liverpool Football Club?"

I said: "Yeh, I do a bit of scouting for them". He said: "You know the Kop? I built it," and he stuck his chest out.

I said: "Did you George?" and he said "Yes. All the steelwork is my job. We followed the design to the letter. We put a roof on that could cover 39,000 people"

I used to go before they put the cover on. In those days you put your cap on and put a paper bag over your head to keep the rain out!

One occasion on the Kop I remember happened during the war. Liverpool were playing Everton in a war-time derby.

Everton were winning 2-0 and we were playing worse than they do today. Liverpool were having a stinker and there were Evertonians near us.

The Kop wasn't full in those days and this Evertonian in front of us kept turning round and saying: "There you are, told yers we'd win," and all that.

He was a bloody nuisance. My brother was with me and he was an expert boxer.

At the end of the match, Everton had won 2-0, and this Evertonian turned round again and was saying: "I told you so".

So my brother whips round, pulls his cap over his eyes and thumps him. The Kop all spilled out and made a ring around them, like they used to do in those days.

My brother takes his coat off and says to me "Hold me coat, Harry, while I do him".

This bloke realises he was serious and changes his tune. "Have a fag, mate, come on, let's be friends".

That was it then, but it was funny when I think back, the Kop all spilling out and making a ring round them.

I've got some wonderful memories of the Kop with all the lads in there together.

The atmosphere changed when Bill Shankly came. Why? Because he was one of the lads himself.

He stood on the Kop, often in an old cap and an old scarf.

Everyone knew he was there and would start shouting 'Shanks is over there'. He'd be singing along with us as well.

There was a great atmosphere at every match. We rarely got beaten but when we did nobody was sorry because we backed Shankly to the hilt. And Bob Paisley, too.

Bob was a lovely man. We got on well together when I was scouting.

I used to go into the players' lounge before the game and when the lads were going in to get changed he'd stay in there and watch the telly.

"Aren't you going in Bob?"

I'd ask.

"Aye, I'll go in for five minutes after," he'd say because the racing was on and he was a fan of that.

He was always backing horses and I said once: "You must be well off by now Bob with all those winners you're backing".

He looked at me and said in his distinctive voice: "I haven't backed a winner yet".

He was smashing. He'd be sat there just before kick-off in an old cloth clap and with his slippers on.

You wouldn't think he was manager of the best team in the world.

As I said, I worked for Liverpool under Bob as a scout. I was brought in by Bill Shankly because I had a good record with a team in the mid-Cheshire league which at that time was part of football's pyramid.

When Bob took over he asked me to carry on because he said Bill had recommended me and Geoff Twentyman.

So I carried on as long as I could and went right through until 1985 under Kenny Dalglish when there were changes and Ron Yeats took over as chief scout.

It's the games I watched on the Kop that my most wonderful memories are from, though.

One game I'll always remember was in 1963 when we played Burnley in an FA Cup replay on a Wednesday night.

The score was one each and it went into extra-time. Liverpool got a penalty in the last minute kicking towards the Kop.

Dead silence. Nobody wanted to take it because it was so important. So Ronnie Moran picked the ball up and his attitude was 'let me take it'.

He didn't take penalties normally but he put it on the spot, walked back, ran up to the ball and cracked it.

He scored and the Kop . . . well, I've never heard a roar like it.

You see, the pubs and clubs used to close at 10 o'clock then. It was quarter-to-ten and it meant we still had to rush down the Kop steps to get a pint.

The referee turned round and blew his whistle to signal the end of the game and we were straight off, running down the Kop steps.

There were some steps on the Kop in those days. There were so many I used to slide down the bannisters sometimes!

Anyway we all went down as quick as we could, out the gate and into the Walker's House next door.

I think we had four pints and were in there to something like 11 o'clock. That was a great night.

I remember watching Wales play Scotland at Anfield. I was in the Paddock that night and even though it was strange watching a game there that didn't involve Liverpool, the atmosphere was still fantastic and still got to me.

The Kop, as it was back then, used to act like an echo. The roar would go out of the ground and you could hear it down at the bottom of Utting Avenue by Broadway.

You could hear the roar from there. Terrific.

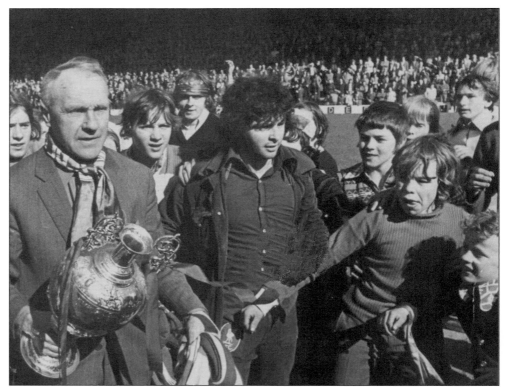

Shanks' ranks: The messiah meets his worshippers

Arise Sir Rednose: Alan Kennedy aka 'Barney Rubble' does the honours in a mock knighthood ceremony with some Kopites during the 1980s

'They gave us a goal start'

You never knew how many were in the old Kop. Allegedly, there were 25,000 but I think there could be more for really big games.

They affectionately nicknamed me 'Barney Rubble', maybe because I played like The Flintstones character; running through walls and giving everything.

They often gave us a goal start on the Kop. They were so vociferous. They used to really chant our names and get behind us. At times that ball used to be sucked into the back of the net. Maybe they came to expect us to win every game at Anfield but sometimes

that wasn't the case. One of the good things about it was they always gave the opposing goalkeeper a round of applause. In 1981/82, when we won the league against Tottenham, Ray Clemence came back and they gave him a great round of applause. I think that gees goalkeepers up.

Does anywhere else compare with the Kop? Not in this country. We played against Benfica in the Stadium of Light and that was a bit intimidating. It was a very high stadium, with 120,000 people. When people saw all those people on the Kop, the hair stood up on the back of the neck.

I'm sure some just froze at Anfield but it often also brought out the best in people.

'The Mersey beat and how the Kop became a stage of its own'

Only very rarely is the Anfield Spion Kop ever accorded anything approaching a true representation of its real stature.

Sure there will likely always remain a broad perception of its prominence, yet any attempt at conveying fully the essence of the Kop and its impact on modern football culture is inclined to fall someway short of its target.

Fact is with something so ethereal as the Spion Kop, mere words are never enough.

Back in 1964 the reporter for the BBC Panorama documentary covering what in those days was termed the 'Kop phenomenon' probably came as near as anybody to defining that essence.

Standing awestruck in front of the baying, swaying massed terrace prior to the 1964 title clincher against Arsenal he remarked briefly yet accurately how 'the Kop didn't behave like any other football crowd'.

Within his simple yet insightful statement perhaps lies the key to understanding just what the Anfield Spion Kop was about and how it came to revolutionise football culture.

Today, of course, we take for granted the modern global spectacle the game has become.

The singing, the chanting, the

A new striker? Shanks with Cilla Black as the Merseybeat took hold on and off the pitch

flags and the colour have become so integral a part of football that it is nigh impossible for most to envisage a time when such partisanship wasn't part of the scene.

Curiously, in Britain at least, that time was actually not so long before those Panorama cameras visited Anfield.

If the phenomenon the BBC news team came to witness that afternoon did not exactly happen overnight then it certainly only became prominent once that particular championship-winning season approached its climax.

Until that little period of football history in the making, the Spion Kop was, in truth, little different from any other crowded terrace.

Possibly its patrons may have been slightly more exuberant and boisterous than most.

Perhaps, too, more prone to sporadic outbursts and isolated chants from the odd cluster of fans.

For the most part, however, everything was - collectively speaking - restrained and orderly.

Essentially, a gathering of like-minded enthusiastic individuals rather than the single homogenous excitable mass into which it was so ▶

Glimpse of the heroes: A young Kopite peers round a towering steel pylon as he desperately seeks an unusual view of the action in April, 1964

> rapidly to evolve. So what happened to transform things?

Well, this was early Sixties Liverpool we must remember. A post-war Liverpool that history confirms was a fertile cradle of exceptional creativity and initiative. And fast fulfilling it, too.

The Beatles had just emerged as the worldwide acclaimed vanguard of a veritable reservoir of talent - gumption too - that was to go on to permeate a broad spectrum of prime British cultural and business strata for several decades to come.

Released from the grievous restraints of war that had dogged preceding generations and fuelled by the increasing Sixties affluence that offered a diversion away from the drudgery of the workplace, the natural wit and exuberance of the Scouser suddenly found itself all manner of platforms on which to express that latent talent.

As it so happened - with the exception of the Fab Four's unique worldwide arena - the Anfield Spion Kop became the biggest stage of them all. Certainly it was the loudest. As the Mersey Sound resonated around the world, the full throttle of 28,000 of its own kind promptly amplified it.

Cocooned and isolated in a way you could never get today, the patrons of the Kop simply did what came naturally to them and - amongst other more base tendencies - swayed and sang along heartily with the pre-match tannoy. Here the Liverpool Irish pub sing-song culture was clearly to play a significant role.

Not many of the Kopites at the time were exactly strangers to belting out a communal tune from the comfort of their own ale-house on a Saturday night. The Kop simply became a giant extension of that concept. Soon more traditional melodies were hijacked and revamped with Liverpudlian lyrics reflecting the local vernacular and humour.

In no time at all, without any contrivance, all the ingredients were in place. Almost if not quite overnight it seemed the Kop had become a completely distinct and separate entity to all its peer terraces.

Those orthodox and orderly flat cap characteristics of football crowds that had prevailed since the game's inception were now rendered old hat. The Spion Kop had found a culture all its own and was ready to unleash it on an unsuspecting audience.

In some ways what happened on the Kop can be viewed as a leap of creativity not dissimilar and certainly not unconnected to the spark that was igniting popular music around the same time.

Sure there was an element of evolution present yet what stands out above all is that impression of originality and spontaneity. What had taken place had been instinctive. Most certainly it was something to be cherished.

At this point, I'd like if I may to draw another musical analogy with what took place back then on the Spion Kop. I dare say some might consider it a somewhat tenuous one. Personally, however, I think it helps illustrate quite aptly the central point I'm trying to make about what transpired.

There's a song featured at the end of the film 'The Big Lebowski' as the credits are rolling. The song is 'Viva Las Vegas' by the new country blues artist Shawn Colvin.

It's taken from the 1995 tribute album to the acclaimed song-smith Doc Pomus who some thirty years earlier had been co-writer of the song with his writing partner, Mort Shuman. The original version you may recall was the title track for the 1964 film starring Elvis Presley.

That original Elvis interpretation had been quirky and upbeat, sprinkled with Hollywood-style pep and glitz. More than thirty other artists went on to record the song after Elvis. Each adheres fairly faithfully to the Elvis interpretation.

Mercifully, Shawn Colvin's version is the one refreshing and compelling exception. In Colvin's take the protagonist becomes as reckless and mysterious as the original was cheery and predictable.

Beguiling us to accompany her into those darker ruinous corners of addiction and obsessiveness that seam through Las Vegas, Colvin manages somehow to re-invent the song, bringing out hitherto concealed beauty and starkness of melody and lyric alike.

Her vocal innovation redefines the parameters of what Pomus and Shuman had written, giving us something completely distinctive; three or four smouldering minutes to savour.

The Kop's early Sixties spark of Scouse invention and innovation managed to pull off a similar trick to Colvin with regard to our spectatorial habits and, ultimately, our footballing culture.

In a way Shawn Colvin was to do with her song interpretation years later - though with the accent firmly on Scouse chirpiness as distinct from Colvin's

Star of the '60s: The man for whom the original 'St John handclap' was born, as the Kop follows the action on a snowy Anfield day

Nevada darkness - it saw the Spion Kop redefine the parameters of football support.

Where once had been a banked dreary terrace no different to so many others, there was now a world-renowned and oft-imitated shrine where a congregation gathered to pay homage and sing its team's praises.

Individual voices may have paled next to Shawn Colvin's.

Yet together in communion, those voices were even more exquisite.

Like with Colvin's song, the Kop's hitherto obscured beauty was able to blossom. Every other Saturday it afforded us not three or four but ninety or more life-affirming minutes to savour.

> 'Where once had been a banked dreary terrace, there was now a world-renowned and oft-imitated shrine where a congregation gathered to pay homage'

On top of the world: A view from the top of the Kop in the early 1960s, with the Sandon pub in the distance – where an historic meeting saw the birth of Liverpool Football Club at Anfield. Right: The Kop steps from the same era, a sea of rooftops to the left

Thousands were locked out of the ground at Anfield today when the gates were closed at 1.45pm with a capacity crowd inside to watch the league championship decision between Liverpool and Arsenal.

A police official said: "It's worse than we expected," and by 12:30pm traffic was building up to a complete block.

Hundreds of motorists were parking their cars miles from the ground and making their way to the turnstiles on foot.

Scenes bordering on chaos were reported at 1:30pm when thousands of vehicles were pouring into the vicinity of the ground.

Mounted police were busy controlling the crowds and other police were being reinforced by members of the special constabulary, said a police spokesman.

At 1pm a police spokesman from E Division at Westminister Road said: "We have every available man at Anfield and we are fully extended".

From 1:45pm onwards the ground was tightly packed with an exultant singing crowd waiting for kick off.

"They're just singing their heads off - they love it," said an official. "But," he added, "with this big crowd it looks like being about 5pm before the ground is cleared".

The turnstiles at Anfield were opened at 12:50pm for the big game against Arsenal.

By the time the gates opened the approaching streets were jammed with football fans.

Lake Street, for instance, was packed 15 to 20 deep with queuing fans.

Thousands of fans surrounded the ground as late as 12:30pm, pouring out of taxis and off buses knowing full well they hadn't a chance of getting in.

"We know we haven't got a chance but we couldn't take the risk. We may get in," was the comment of one optimistic Wavertree fan.

The queue started to form as early as 10 o'clock last night but by 9 o'clock this morning there were still only 50 fans outside.

Title joy: The good news from Anfield on April 18, 1964

People coming out of nearby public houses after closing time last night were staggered to see the fans armed with transistor radio sets, camp beds and flasks of hot coffee arriving at the Spion Kop end of the ground for the long vigil.

The fans kept lively by singing 'Oh When the Saints Go Marching In' and shouting other football slogans.

First in the queue were 17-year-old Collegiate schoolboy George Hunter of Russell Road, Mossley Hill, and his friend, Alan Wilcock, also 17, of Holbeck Street, Anfield.

By midnight the queue had grown to about 20 strong.

Ticket holders found great difficulty in reaching their sections of the ground as the crowds surged from gate to gate in an endeavour to join the shortest queue. When one gate was closed there was a concentrated rush to other sections of the ground.

Many people who arrived to find milling mobs of people besieging all the entrances decided to call it a day. They then trekked across Stanley Park to watch Everton's reserve game against Barnsley at Goodison Park.

**FROM 'THOUSANDS LOCKED OUT AT ANFIELD',
Liverpool Echo, Saturday, April 18, 1964**

I've never heard a noise like the Kop made that afternoon. It made you want to stop and listen to them calling for their team to win.

**GEOFF STRONG (who was playing for
Arsenal on the day)**

We were on top of the world as we did a lap of honour at the end. I was so full of joy that I could have played another 90 minutes.

ROGER HUNT (Liverpool striker)

'Do you want your gate money or just cash from the empty bottles?'

As a young teenager in the post-war football boom, I lived very near the ground. In those days many fans cycled to the games.

I was able to earn a pound or two, storing bicycles on match days.

It became my habit to join the small crowd outside the big gates at the Kemlyn corner of the Kop waiting for them to open at three-quarter time.

As soon as being admitted it was a dash up the steps to crane a neck over the crowd to catch a glimpse of my heroes - Billy Liddell, Albert Stubbins and also to see Cyril Sidlow, the Welsh international goalkeeper in action, as I had a particular interest in goalkeepers.

Judging the time finely, a few minutes before the end of the game, a dash was made back down the steps to get home in time to give out the bikes.

A match, which stands out in my mind, illustrates the difference between the old Kop and the present stand.

Liverpool met Glasgow Celtic in the second leg of the European Cup Winners Cup on April 19th, 1966. The first leg on the 14th in Glasgow was lost by 1-0 and the Celtic supporters were confident of a victory.

After all, no team had scored more than one goal against them in this competition. We were sure of going through to the final.

Why? Because Shanks had said so.

The Celtic supporters started arriving in the morning for the evening game and were drifting around the ground carrying their 'liquid' refreshment.

A few were so 'tired' that they missed the game, sleeping it off in the streets outside.

About two hours before kick-off I joined the crowd opting to use the turnstiles in the centre of the Kop as the queues were heavy up Kemlyn Road.

There was no real attempt by the police at crowd control, only to keep the main road free for traffic.

There was a great press of humanity around the four gates, pushing and shoving to get near a gate, the crowd would surge and we would be swept past to start again from the other side.

Eventually getting in, a programme was bought from a man with a satchel, price four (old) pence.

The many steps up to the top were climbed (I never did count these), paused at the top to look back at the panoramic view of the city before turning again to see the best view in the world - Anfield from the very back of the Kop.

Down the terracing to the usual spec in the middle and soon joined by a small group of fans from Hull who travelled to every game by mini-van. A shilling sweep was organised for the first goal scorer. Sir Roger was not playing so chances would be even. I drew the goalkeeper!

Calm after the storm: Police look on

Banter was starting up and the solitary jovial policeman walked up and down behind the Kop goal.

Beatlemania was in full swing - 'We Love You, yeah, yeah, yeah!' The Celtic crowd, seemingly many more than their 5,000 allocation, waved green and white flags chanting 'Celtic, Celtic', the

Kop replying with 'Rangers' and 'go back to Ireland'.

An hour to go before kick off and the Kop was jammed packed with 28,000 fans.

No chance of getting out.

There were no refreshment bars or betting kiosks anyway. At last the heroes appeared on the field to a tumultuous welcome.

Names were chanted - Lawrence, Lawler, Byrne, Milne, Yeats, Stevenson, Callaghan, Strong, St John, Smith, Thompson.

It was soon clear that the game would be a bruising battle. Tommy Smith hit the post and Chris Lawler of all people, missed from close in.

Soon after the half-hour Geoff Strong badly injured his knee and could only hobble about. Lennox missed a good chance for Celtic. Half-time passed with no goals scored.

With time passing the crowd roared the team on: 'Attack, Attack, Attack'.

Smith had been fouled heavily a couple of times and on the second occasion, just after the hour, he rose up to hit the free kick into the corner of the net to rapturous applause.

A few minutes later a dribble by Thompson, a through ball to Cally and an immaculate centre for Strong to leap up on his one leg to head the ball past Simpson.

A nerve wracking 20 minutes to go. Celtic got the ball into the net but the offside flag was up much to the relief of the home side and the ire of the away fans, raining bottles down at the Anfield Road end.

A nail biting last couple of minutes and we were through to our very first European final.

Shankly was to remark later to his friend Jock Stein "would he take his share of the gate money or would he prefer to take the cash from the empty bottles".

What of today's stadium?

Now I can put on my coat and scarf with 20 minutes to kick-off, stroll to a turnstile with a small queue and still be at my seat with 10 minutes to spare.

Which would I prefer?

I'll leave you to guess but I will say this - I would not have missed the '60s for the world.

The leaving
of Liverpool:
John Aldridge
runs off the
Anfield pitch
for the last
time as a
Liverpool
player after
throwing his
shirt and
boots into
the Kop after
the 9-0
demolition of
Crystal
Palace in
1989

Right: An
Aldo goal at
the Kop end
against
Nottingham
Forest

'We were **4-0 down** and all I **could hear** was them singing 'Aldo is a **Kopite!'**

I started off on the Kop in the boys' pen and I can remember one funny incident that happened to me.

I was about 13 and at the time I had very long hair. I was down right at the front of the Kop and behind me was this big bloke, a docker or a bouncer or something.

Every time the Kop surged forward I could feel him pressed right up against me. I was worried he was going to roll up an Echo and p*** down my leg but when the surge stopped he moved back a bit and said to me 'sorry, love'. He thought I was a bird! I'll tell you something, I got rid of that haircut straight away after that! There was no danger of me going on the Kop again with long hair.

I had some great nights on the Kop though. St Etienne and the Bruges game, the one when we came back from two goals down in the UEFA Cup Final, they're the ones that really stick in my mind. Some of the derby games too. It really was the place to be.

It was dangerous at times. You'd get pushed around and there were always people who would pass out and get passed down to the front over people's heads. It was magic though, different class. There's never been anywhere to match it and never will.

For me, the Kop was unique. Everyone remembers the footage of them singing the Beatles songs and the atmosphere on there was terrific. I'm all for all-seater stadia but the atmosphere isn't the same now.

I can well remember the first time I played in front of the Kop. It was brilliant. I was playing for Oxford United at the time and before the game I went on Football Focus and did a piece with them where I said what a big Liverpool fan I was.

We got tonked that afternoon. Liverpool were magnificent. It was 6-0 and I think Rushie got two. I got a great reception from the Kop though and I think we were about 4-0 down and all I could hear was them singing 'Aldo is a Kopite'. That was really nice. I really appreciated it.

I think I summed up what the Kop and those who stood on it meant to me in my final game for Liverpool. It was the night we beat Crystal Palace 9-0 and I scored a penalty after Kenny brought me on. I hadn't planned it, it was totally off the cuff, but I threw my shirt and my boots into the Kop. I didn't want to leave Liverpool and I know that they didn't want me to go either. It was a very emotional night for me.

JOHN ALDRIDGE

I obviously knew about the Kop before I had signed for Liverpool. It has always been something special, especially when it was a standing area.

To my knowledge, the only other place where you would get 26,000 people standing behind a goal like that was at Borussia Dortmund.

Liverpool, as a club, is something special to me. That's probably because I signed for them as a fan. And my first real experience of the Kop as a player was fantastic.

When I started the game against Leeds and I heard everyone singing 'You'll Never Walk Alone', I felt as though I was 2m10 instead of 1m90. It made me feel very proud, because the people there were singing with their hearts. The Liverpool fans were always great to me. I got a good reaction from them, which is something every player looks for. That's what makes football special.

ERIK MEIJER

Guess who? Tony Hateley finds the net for Liverpool against
Walsall in the 1960s – not that the Kop knew anything about it!

'The Kop chanted 'who scored?' and back from the Annie Road came the reply: 'Tony Hateley!"

THE FANS
We are the famous,
the famous Kopites

When we were young and couldn't afford to get in, we used to climb into the Kop over the wall. We'd end up with cut hands and all the rest of it but that didn't matter. We just wanted to get in.

I'd go with my mates - Billy and Teddy Molyneux, Billy, Paul and Jimmy Collins and Charlie Daly.

Once we were in there was these shrubs inside the ground and we'd go and hide in them.

About an hour before kick-off this 'arl fella would come along and start swinging a big stick into the bushes. We'd be getting smacked in the head, arms and everywhere else but none of us would shout out because if he found us we'd end up getting chucked out.

Once he'd gone we'd go into the Kop and watch the game. The Kop was great. People really would just take a p*** wherever they were stood.

There was talk about you being able to see the steam coming off the Kop from the heat but it wasn't that, it was the steam from the p*** hitting the concrete.

I remember when I started in the boys' pen. There'd be all kinds of scraps in there. We'd try and get out into the Kop as well. There was a bit where you could squeeze through and get from the pen into the Kop but I was a bit chubby so I'd go over the top.

We weren't hooligans or anything like that but we'd always be getting up to things. There was a lad who'd stand at the front of the Kop selling sweets at games. He was a bit like Everton's Toffee girl I suppose.

Anyway, I remember him getting dragged into the Kop once and we all grabbed as many sweets as we could and then legged off before anything could be done about it.

There were two lads who'd go around tipping (robbing) people. I remember one game when one of these lads suddenly let out a scream. We looked round and on his hand there was a mouse trap!

He'd tried to pickpocket a fella who had clearly been done before and this fella had put a mousetrap into his pocket! That was a classic moment.

There was this other fella who used to go on the Kop called Johnny Walker. He was the lad who used to run on and give Gordon West a handbag.

Anyway, he couldn't always afford to pay to get in so he used to go in The Albert before a game and chew glass for money! He'd hold a collection while he was doing it and then pay to get in.

I remember the time when Man United played Arsenal in a cup game at Anfield. We couldn't let either of them have our Kop so we paid to get in and went and stood right in the centre. There was about 350 of us with all these bizzies around us.

The United fans and the Arsenal fans both tried to get in the centre of the Kop but we wouldn't let them.

It was our Kop and there was no way we were giving it up for them. We'd go to away games when we were kids even though we couldn't afford to go.

We'd get up to Haydock where all the trucks were and we'd ask the drivers where they were going.

Say we'd be trying to get to Highbury we'd get a driver saying 'I can take you as far as Leicester'. We'd be like 'Well that's closer to Highbury then where we are now' and jump on the back.

We'd be under tarpaulin sheets and stuff in the freezing rain or snow going down the motorway on the back of a truck. We were only kids and I suppose we could've been murdered or anything but we didn't think about that. We just wanted to go and see Liverpool play and would do anything to get there.

TOMMY FAIRCLOUGH

My fondest memory of the Kop was when the great man himself, Mr Bill Shankly, stood on the Kop among his fans.

It was during the league game against Notts Forest. The Kop started to chant 'Shankly, Shankly give us a song'. All went quiet...but Shanks just laughed!

It was great to see him standing on the Kop with the fans he dearly loved.

Another great memory is from when Liverpool played Walsall in a FA Cup game at Anfield. The ground was covered in fog and there was a goal scored at the Anfield Road end.

The Kop started chanting 'who scored' and back from the Anfield Road end came 'Tony Hately'.

Straight away back from the Kop came a chant of 'thank you very much for the information'.

Great memories.

JOHN PRITCHARD

I remember the day when we played Norwich on what was the Kop's Last Stand in 1994. I am a season ticket holder and I took my usual standing position on the Kop with my mates and watched the match as usual.

However, after the game, as the crowds were beginning to leave, a fan standing next to us produced a hammer from his coat and proceeded to chip away at the famous steps. He then collected some of the rubble and put it in his pockets.

At this point some stewards and police officers started to move in our direction to help disperse the crowds. Seeing this, one of the culprit's mates' chirped up "Hurry up, before the police collar ya".

He then added, "Just tell 'em you can't arrest me officer because you need some concrete evidence!" This put a smile on all our faces at the end of an historic match that had ended in defeat.

CARL WILLIAMS

Being a 17-year-old Liverpool supporter isn't all fun and games. You have to endure constant reminders of how today's team, the team you follow with a passion, isn't fit to lace the boots of the previous great sides who played under Shankly, Paisley, Fagan and Dalglish.

To me, the eighteen league championships and four European Cups only exist in videos, books and stories told by nostalgic and teary-eyed relatives.

That all changed in season 2000-2001. Gerard Houllier's team ripped through domestic and European opposition with ease. First came the Worthington Cup, then the FA Cup, closely followed by the UEFA Cup, and entry into the oversized piggy-bank that is the Champions League.

It was like nothing I'd ever known.

To me, the names of Hyypia, Gerrard, Hamann, Heskey and Owen are as important as the names of Hansen, Souness, Kennedy, Keegan and Dalglish are to older Reds, and they always will be.

Off the back of that Treble success, the Champions League was negotiated with renewed optimism and hope. In the last game of the second group phase we needed to beat Roma at Anfield by two clear goals to reach the quarter finals.

Little did I know as I took my seat for around the 100th time, that this would be my great night at Anfield. My St Etienne. The whole night started on the best possible note as, emerging from a tunnel filled with photographers to give a bear hug to Roma boss Fabio Capello, was Gerard Houllier, five months after life-saving heart surgery, to heroically lead his team. He couldn't have timed it better.

I still maintain that I was the first in the ground to see him, and as I shouted 'There's Houllier', everyone looked and cheered. The night felt special from that point, as I felt that there was no way we would fail to win this. Not with 'Le Boss' back.

Two of our most influential players, Didi Hamann and Michael Owen were in the stand, suspended and injured respectively. They were not to be needed. This night was to be based on raw emotion.

We flew at the Italians from the start. A great move resulted in Smicer's long range shot being well saved. From the corner, Murphy was fouled.

Penalty. Jari Litmanen. 1-0. Six minutes gone. Could there have been a better start?

Roma were forlorn, the frustrated Francesco Totti couldn't find a way past the barrier of Henchoz and Hyypia. Anfield was rocking, as 'Allez, Allez, Gerard Houllier' rang around each of its four corners, with scarves being twirled in the air.

I knew that I was in the presence of something special but needed that second goal to confirm it.

Just after the hour mark, it arrived.

A free-kick from Murphy was met by a towering header from Heskey. Cue bedlam. I'd never heard a noise like it. In my eyes, Emile Heskey had just become my generation's David Fairclough, the scorer of a goal that, if you were there, you'll never ever forget.

The remaining half an hour or so was a mixture of chanting and singing, nervous tension, then more chanting and singing. I wanted it to end because that meant we'd be through but I

'Little did **I know** as I took my seat that **this** would be my great night at Anfield. My St Etienne . . .'

wanted it to carry on because the place was so alive. I'd happily have stayed there all night.

It did end of course and the final whistle was met with the loudest cheer of all. We'd reached the quarter finals, and everything about the game was perfect.

Houllier's return. The early Litmanen penalty. The fact that it was Heskey, so often criticised, who got the famous goal. That was it then.

I had experienced one of the great European nights and it is a game that will stay with me for the rest of my life.

MARK JONES

The thing I remember most about the old Kop was the way that we'd all stand in a neat line, fan by fan, waiting for the kick off.

That would all change when the Reds scored.

As soon as the ball hit the net those immaculate lines would seem to crumble and fall down like soldiers.

Everybody would go forward towards the front as we cheered, screamed and jumped up and down.

Then we had to march back up to our line again and stand neatly, side by side, waiting for the next goal so we could all fall down to the front again. It didn't matter how close to someone or where you were standing, you'd always end up at the front. It's something I'll always remember.

CAROL BODDINGTON

Whilst a schoolboy, throughout the glorious '80s, I travelled to each home game on the train from North Wales.

Not believing me that the atmosphere on the Kop was like 'being on another planet' for 90 minutes, a number of mates would accompany me to the odd match.

I would make a point that every newcomer had to undergo my self-devised 'reaction test'. I would wait until about quarter to three then proudly lead them in through the turnstiles. I would then lead them up the steps and approach the Kop from the side, past the old

food/drinks bar. At this point, I would make them wait 30 seconds so I could run on ahead and stand just inside the Kop, facing their approach.

When the 'newcomer' appeared around the corner for their first glimpse at a full Kop, I would look directly at the expression on their faces. I instantly knew from that first look whether or not they were permitted to return with me to my other 'planet' across the border.

A group of blokes who stood regularly at this spot must have caught on over the years. Every time I ran ahead of one of my newcomers they would shout: "More fresh blood on the way then, Taff?" Obviously my trialists still had to master the art of getting behind the goal, half-way up the Kop, but that's someone else's story! Twenty years on and I'm now a season ticket holder in the Main Stand but before each match, I look over to the Kop and think to myself 'I wonder, just wonder, whether there is someone over there who has just passed the same reaction test?'

PAUL HUGHES

One of the best bits of song improvisation I heard on the Kop was against Aston Villa in the early '90s.

The Villa fans had been droning on with their 'ooh-ah Paul McGrath, ooh-ah Paul McGrath' song which goes on and on and on and sounds like that hymn.

Anyway, Jamie Redknapp completely skins him and scores a beauty. After the celebrations die down the Kop finally shut the Villa fans up with their own rendition of the song. It just started off as: 'Where was Paul McGrath? Where was Paul McGrath?'

That was funny in itself but then a new verse was added: 'He was in the bar, he was in the bar,' being a reference to his reputation as a drinker. But then the piece de resistance at the end was the closing line of: 'Jamie Redknapp . . . super-star!' It was an absolutely brilliant piece of instant creativity, unique to the Kop and the best bit was the collective laugh at the end as we all stood there thoroughly pleased with ourselves.

PETER SHARPLES

Those were the days: Clearly the Echo had more than one use as this fan shows as he celebrates another title coming to Anfield with a home-made banner in 1973. Below right: Liver birds on the pitch?

The 1991/92 season wasn't a great one for Liverpool but there were some memorable moments on the Kop.

The sweetest was when Rushie finally nailed the Mancs and their title pretensions, leaving us singing 'You'll never win the league' with, what was at the time, total conviction.

The stand-out memory that year though happened at a half-hearted end of season home defeat to Wimbledon in the league, the night before the General Election.

During a quiet moment in play, a lone voice sang out: "If you're all voting Tory, all voting Tory, all voting Tory you're a ****!"

Must've been those Kemlyn Roaders who got Major re-elected!

The three thousand or so non-season ticket specs for the Kop's 'Last Stand' against Norwich in 1993/94 were naturally like gold-dust but thanks to the persistence of my old fella (an Evertonian, no less!), I eventually managed to obtain one of those precious orange briefs.

The day itself was a bit of blur but what remains clear in the mind is that the excuse for a match being played in front of us barely detracted from the genuinely unforgettable sense of occasion and history.

The full repertoire of old songs, flags, scarves and other paraphernalia were on proud display but it was particularly the pre-match ceremony on the pitch that heightened the feeling that we were part of something truly unique, that would live on however we were housed.

Many famous names from years past were welcomed rapturously on to the pitch but the ear-splitting roar for King Kenny coupled with the singing as Joe Fagan walked out with Nessie Shankly and Jessie Paisley will live with me, and I'm sure many others, forever.

DAN KAY

Bill Shankly's testimonial match in 1975 is one that stands out in my mind. I was totally bemused, numb, when Bill announced his retirement. It was like someone had died, someone important. I was 15 years of age and the lads from my dad's Sunday team had offered me a lift to the game.

It was a total sell-out. Thousands of people locked out and rightly so. We played a Don Revie XI (I think?) and back then Liverpool were always better than England. To be honest the game was incidental. Before the game the Kop was in full voice, new flags and banners paid homage to (Sir) Bill Shankly. Just before the teams came out and YNWA started, Bill started talking over the PA system. The ground fell silent immediately.

I'm sure there was no introduction. You know 'Ladies and Gentleman, Bill Shankly'. That was typical Shanks. No fuss. He spoke and thanked us for all we'd done for him and Liverpool. The result didn't matter but we roared Liverpool on, like it was a derby.

The final whistle blew and it was over, quite literally, over. The players shook hands and applauded the crowd, Bill did a lap of honour. There were no tears from Bill but oceans of tears from every other part of the ground. Some managed to break free from the police and stewards and ran on to the pitch. They shook his hands and draped scarves around his neck.

He stopped and picked every scarf up. They kissed his feet. This was a messiah, and a man of the people, for the people. Shanks went down the tunnel, and everyone bar the Kop left the ground. We stood there and sang and sang for Shankly (The Amazing Grace tune). Then I saw him. He must have come back up into the directors box, climbing over the press box and walked along the Main Stand. He stood there, his hands clasped like in prayer. We sang and sang his name, tears blinding us. Then, he held his hand in the air, turned and walked back. We were emotionally broken. Boys became men and men were reduced to tearful boys. I had to run like the wind back to the car. I was using up their valuable drinking time. I told the lads Shanks had come back to see us. They were gutted they never stayed. It's my worst memory of being on the Kop but the most emotional and memorable.

MARK GRIMES

What was better than a Saturday afternoon standing in the middle of the Spion Kop? Jostling your way into the middle, where the singing and atmosphere was; the songs, the swaying the atmosphere. It was second to none.

My memories of the Kop include the 3-3 draw with Man Utd and the 'parting of the red sea'. It was 3-2 to Man U at the time when suddenly I felt a little unwell! I shouted out to everyone around me that I was going to be sick and like the parting of the sea a space appeared as if from nowhere.

Seconds before we were all arm to arm, snuggled in, and then I was able to walk straight down the middle of the Kop to the St John Ambulance men at the front, where I was allowed to cool down before watching Razor Ruddock hammer an unstoppable header into the Anfield Road end past a helpless Peter Schmeichel.

Another memory was the victory against Auxerre when even though the Kop was only half full the atmosphere was second to none. It was freezing but being in the middle of the Spion Kop generated enough heat to keep us warm. Mark Walters' goal, and his classic step-over, might not go down as one of the most explosive moments in LFC history but oh, what a memory.

And then of course there was the Kop's Last Stand versus Norwich City. Four of us jostled our way into the Kop. One lad had a cast on his leg. By the end everyone agreed that it will be missed forever, nearly as much as my mate's cast was. It had come off during the jostling of the match! Nobody was hurt but this is surely one of the maddest things that had ever happened to someone.

STEVE DEVINE

I remember the time the Kop actually chanted Everton! It sounds like it can't be true but it was. It was a night match against Coventry City in 1977 in the old League Cup. There were Coventry fans in the Kemlyn Road stand right by the Kop. Somehow Coventry managed to score which was unusual in those days. Everton had just beaten Coventry 6-0 and when they started chanting '1-0' we all started chanting 'Everton'. It was loud and I'm still washing my mouth out with soap to this day!

FRANK WALKER

I remember that famous night we beat St Etienne in March 1977. At that time, I used to travel to Liverpool from my home in Birmingham on the train. I was 17, just started work, and used to spend most of my £19 weekly wages on following the Reds.

That day, I caught the midday train to Lime Street and arrived at the ground at around 3.30pm. Some lads I used to meet on the train from Bristol joined me in the Sandon for some pre-match beverages. We used to cram into the tiny little room on the side of the pub.

At around 5.30pm someone came in and said the queues were all around the ground, so we decided to join the fray, in case it was a lock-out. From then on, with the French in their bright green wigs and swaying crowd outside the ground, it became my most memorable occasion of following the mighty Reds. I stood around the middle of the Kop and when the teams came out it was incredible. I'm sure the crowd blew Keegan's cross into the net after a minute.

Gradually though, it dawned on us that this French team were no pushovers and when they equalised, it was pretty much deserved. The Kop once again showed why we have the greatest reputation for getting behind our team and willed Razor's goal to drag ourselves back. Then the moment that anyone who was there will surely put in their top 10 moments of life itself. Supersub scored. I will never forget the second it happened. We held our breath before he struck the ball. We knew this was it - the end of our dream if he missed, the realisation of our dream if it went in. Sure, there were more rounds to play but St Etienne were the best team left in the cup.

All I remember about the madness when it went in was . . . I lost my shoe! My brown platform heeled shoe shot off my foot, never to be seen again. I waited until the crowd cleared and looked everywhere for it before happily resigning myself to limping home to Birmingham with one shoe. I had to catch the last train to Crewe at around 11.45pm, wait for a train to Rugby at around 1am, sleep at Rugby for a couple of hours then catch a mail train to Birmingham arriving at 6am. I would then go straight to work because I started at 7am. When I limped into work with one shoe I was still on cloud nine and no amount of mickey-taking could alter my mood.

MEL FREEMAN

Full house: The Kop overflows as 55,232 turn up to watch Liverpool return to the top of the Second Division table after a 2-0 defeat of Blackburn Rovers in 1957.

Bye, bye, bye, bye: The Kop (left) shows its approval as Carlton Palmer is dismissed in August '93
Hat-trick: Although the lad at the front reckons it was only two!

The first game I actually stood on the Kop for was Chris Lawler's testimonial.

I don't remember anything at all about it though, apart from that I had to sit on the barrier to actually see.

Talking of barriers, the amount of times you got pushed off and then back on was unbelievable. Sometimes your legs would go numb and you were desperate not to get pushed off as you wouldn't be able to stand.

I then moved on to a milk crate in front of the barriers. This was pretty safe but was a chore walking to the ground having to carry it.

I always enjoyed night matches at Anfield, especially the European games. I took a day off school and went with my dad to queue down Kemlyn Road for tickets for the return leg against Forest in '78/79.

We lost the first game 2-0 and although we had most of the game that night, we just couldn't score at Anfield. Forest were a good side then though.

The Kop used to have a great rapport with Peter Shilton. 'Tina, Tina, Tina' we'd shout at him and 'We all agree Clemo is better than Tina'. He always took it in good humour though.

Around the early '80s, Ipswich were one of our main rivals and we had a couple of seasons when we played them in the League Cup.

I think one of those was when Mark Lawrenson made a tackle from behind on the penalty spot when an Ipswich forward, could have been Mariner or Gates, was through on goal. It was the best executed tackle I've ever seen.

I think it was in one of these games in the cup against Arsenal that went to extra-time and me and my mate nipped out to the chippy behind the Kop for a split and gravy, then back into the Kop to watch extra time with our chips!

Around this time there was talk of Eric Gates coming to Anfield in place of Craig Johnston and I remember the song "We all agree Skippy is better than Wurzel". One enjoyable afternoon was the time we beat Man United 4-0 in 1990. Their favourite song at the time was 'Always look on the bright side of life' but when the fourth goal went in the whole of Anfield sang it back to them. It was immense, even the Kemlyn Road were singing it. I've still got it on tape.

**Gizza hand up:
This was a familiar
sight in the '50s and
'60s. It's grown men
climbing over, not
excited youngsters!**

Going to Anfield was a fantastic experience for me. I first stood on the Kop when I was seven and coming from Canvey Island in Essex I did not realise that my accent was not Scouse.

All my family on my mum's side lived on the Wirral and going to Anfield was a real family occasion. We would get the ferry across to the Pier Head and the bus up to Anfield.

Once in Anfield I would be dropped off in the boys' pen while my uncles took their place in the Kop half way up behind the goal. It was at half-time when the police were not looking that I would climb over the fence and find my uncles.

For me, the noise and fans were incredible. The sheer volume was consuming and it was something that I looked forward to.

The humour of the Kop was something that I picked up on very quickly and the thing that stood out for me was in 1976 when we played Barcelona in the 2nd leg of the UEFA Cup semi-final.

We had beaten Barca at the Nou Camp 1-0 with a John Toshack goal. On the return all I heard about was Johan Cruyff this and Johan Cruyff that so when I went to Anfield I was expecting to see some kind of God.

Half way through the game the ball was played to Cruyff who was on the side of the pitch by the Kemlyn Road (now Centenary) Stand when he went to control the ball and it went straight under his foot for a Liverpool throw.

Straight away one Kopite shouted out '10 grand a week?'

And what about that huge tin of Crown Paint they used to put on the centre spot when Liverpool were sponsored by them? About a dozen men used to get hernias carting it off before the game started. That always used to give us a laugh on the Kop.

**KEITH
CUNLIFFE**

'More like 10 lots of s***e a week' and everyone around us cracked up laughing.

For me though, the Kop was all about passion and support for Liverpool and when we sang it was all as one.

**ANDREW
HOUSE**

When we were kids we went in the boys' pen. Going in there when you were aged nine or 10 was sort of taking a step into the Kop. It had barbed wire on the top with remains of clothes where boys had escaped out of there to actually get on the Kop. One of the bars was bent on the boys' pen but they used to put a Copper on duty there because you could squeeze through when you were little.

It was a mad place to be though. There were girders on the top, part of the framework, and lads used to get up there from the boys' pen and walk along them. You'd see people above you walking along the girders. There have been stories which have changed over the years about Bill Shankly going on the Kop after he had retired.

Someone said that he went on in disguise. He never. Imagine Shankly doing that. He wasn't that type of fella. He'd also go to Everton and Man United games after he'd retired where he was treated as a VIP but at Liverpool they didn't allow him near the players so, even though he was Liverpool's greatest manager, he went on the Kop as a fan. That showed what an exceptional person he was.

I was there the day when Shankly actually went on the Kop. It was in November 1975, after he had retired, and I was 15 at the time.

We played Coventry at home and drew 1-1. I used to get in the Kop early and I remember there was a bit of excitement in there. There was a bit of a buzz and they were all singing Shankly's name.

When a player's name got sung you'd see all the arms go up and point towards the pitch where the player was. This time the arms were all pointing from both directions on the Kop to the centre.

Apparently Shankly was on there and was getting shoved all over the place, from pillar to post.

When things had settled down I remember that he actually stayed on there for well over half an hour. I remember there was a fella who stood by him right through the game who had a red jumper on.

The reason I remember it so well is that I actually shook hands with him. I shook hands with Bill Shankly on the Kop.

That was unbelievable because I was only 15 and I'll always remember it.

ANTHONY RADCLIFFE

I believe we were playing Man United during the great season of '89. Manchester fans were booing the ref for making some calls in Liverpool's favour.

They started to loudly chant 'Who's the Scouser in the black?' Without missing a beat, the Kop responded with a thunderous roar . . . 'Johnny Barnes, Johnny Barnes, Johnny Barnes', to which the away supporters were silenced. John Barnes clapped his hands to the Kop to show his support. You see it wasn't just the cheering and singing that made the Kop the Kop, it was the sense of humour. It didn't matter how the team was doing, someone in the crowd always said something to make the fans smile.

JAMAR KING

I live now in a city in Canada that has the same name that I used to chant as a young lad on the Kop - Saint John. One of my greatest memories of the Spion Kop is from 1966, when Liverpool hosted Ajax of Amsterdam in a European Cup second leg tie.

Liverpool started the game 5-1 down from the first leg. I was 14 at the time and after surviving the crush at the turnstiles (thanks to a large gentleman who put his legs against the wall and his back against the crowd while shouting "there's a lad here, back off will yiz,") I took my place on the Kop to the left of the goal on the same side as the boys' pen.

The attendance was 50,000 plus and the pitch was barely visible due to a thick fog. The Kop amused themselves by blowing in unison, probably after chanting something like '1-2-3 (puff)' to blow the fog away!

It wasn't long before the crush became too much for many in my area. I was near the front and many were being helped out onto the cinder track. One of the first aiders was at the front helping to pull people out and tried to help me out but I was wedged in firmly. I managed to crawl out under my own steam and the next thing I know is we are all being herded along the track. Good, I thought, we are being moved to another spot. Then the door opened and we were out in the parking lot. Anyway I got the bus home, and watched some of the game on TV if I remember correctly. Happy days.

ALAN POWELL

STEPHEN DONE

Liverpool Football Club
Museum Curator

'That flagpole is a symbol still standing proudly'

Behind the Kop stands a giant flagpole. It's a real piece of history, being one of the masts from the famous Great Eastern ship built by world famous engineer Brunel.

The ship, a piece of real maritime history, ended up in the docks at Rock Ferry and when the Kop was being redeveloped as a formal standing area in 1906, someone had the tremendous idea to bring the mast to Anfield and erect it as an enormous flagpole.

The mast had to be floated across the Mersey before being hauled up to Anfield on a wagon pulled by three horses.

They went via Everton Brow and that must have been a real effort up that steep hill.

For me, that flagpole is a symbol of the Kop, still standing proudly close on a century on.

The Kop is actually about people and it remains a very special place for those who sit in it and visit it.

Flying the flag through the ages: The Kop's famous flagpole in 1967 and still standing in later days, as it is now

'How a cop made the Kop

I started off on the Kop standing in the boys' pen. They won the cup in 1965 and at the start of the following season they played Honved, a Hungarian army team.

What was the boys' pen like? Violent! I also remember as a kid standing on the Kop. It was common for the bobbies, wearing those long rain-coats, to be spat upon, although thankfully I've never experienced this myself.

You would see the odd policeman there and his coat would be showered in saliva. It was horrible, absolutely horrible, and thankfully I was never subjected to that.

I joined the police in the 1970s and in the late 1980s I was an inspector in the mounted section. At the Kop end they had cash gates.

This was all pre-Hillsborough and now it's very rare to have cash turnstiles but back then the Lake Street gates, and at flagpole corner, were cash gates.

I remember being in the mounted, not long having been in the department, and cutting my teeth on learning to control the queues. You'd get down to Kemlyn Road and Lake Street for 12.30pm on a Saturday afternoon and the queues were 100 yards long then and five deep.

That was just the norm. If there's any sign of anything near that now we start to get a bit fidgety.

Some of the old mounted police officers were very sophisticated riders and would shout at people. The crowds would just accept this and do as they were told.

An awful lot of football supporters are not frightened of making their feelings known and can be quite stubborn when they want to but they can be very, very co-operative too.

We had one game, I think it was the Auxerre game, when someone collapsed on the Kop.

A chap had suffered a heart attack and the paramedics wanted to get to him. I made a PA announcement to allow them to get through and it was like the parting of the Red Sea. The crowd themselves made a corridor for the paramedics to get through to treat this chap. The Kop can be very co-operative when they want to.

I was at Hillsborough as a fan. I was in the stand above the Leppings Lane end. When I started to do my current job with Terry McKenna in the early 1990s, the Kop was still terraced and at the back was a narrow corridor, like a pathway, where the toilets were. It was scary, particularly on night matches in the winter when it was wet and pitch-black.

There were steps that went down from this corridor at the back of the Kop and it was scary. I looked at them and thought this is not nice. This is dangerous and has got to be changed or there could be a problem.

Things have changed and changed for the better. We don't get people who've passed out with exhaustion or have fainted and been passed to the front now.

Air force: Heads up for (from left) John Rothwell, Ken Keys and Bernie Swift on the Kop in August '91

part like the Red Sea'

Pitching in: It's all hands on deck as St John Ambulance men and police help put an injured fan on to a stretcher as the Kop overspills in December, 1966

People would go to the match then and just accept that's the way it is, but now, the least thing that happens at a football match, a letter will come in or go to the club's safety officer.

For obvious reasons, April and May 1989 was quite a traumatic time. In the last week of the season we had West Ham at Anfield on the Tuesday night and then Arsenal on the Friday.

During the West Ham game, bearing in mind it wasn't that long after Hillsborough, a fire alarm went off inside the ground.

So the story goes, and this is probably exaggerated and is in no way a slur, the fire brigade turned up to investigate what happened to be a false alarm.

They turned up at the wrong place though, the wrong rendezvous point, and thought the best way to get in was through a turnstile.

Apparently the turnstile operator wouldn't let them in unless they each paid £15! They finally get in and the police commander sees the fire brigade officer.

"Where's the nearest fire hydrant?" says the fire brigade officer. "I've not got a clue," replies the police commander. "Well you should know," he says to which the police commander replies: "How many cells are there at Lower Lane Police Station?" "I don't know," says the fire brigade officer. "Well, you should do!"

I know we laugh and joke about the things that have happened on the Kop over the years but we're not complacent. Ray Edwards and Terry McKenna do a hell of a lot of work here and the football is relentless. We love it but we can switch between the social side of it and the work side.

BERNIE SWIFT

I've been doing football matches for 31 seasons now, which is a long time. I retire this year so this is my last season and I can see the way things, not just the Kop, have improved.

The seats mean there is not the same movement. People used to get injured and would faint or get pressed against a barrier and hurt.

The way the Kop used to be, if someone felt unwell in the centre part, they'd lift them up and carry them down on a sea of hands to the front where they'd receive first aid.

On a cold day the warmest place on the Kop was right at the back. If you were on duty at the back of it, as well as getting all the smoke coming back from cigarettes, you'd get all the heat coming back too.

In contrast, if you were working down the front in what was the old 'moat' it was absolutely freezing.

The big downside of the Kop was the toilet facilities. They were useless.

Of course before the game everyone would go and have a couple of pints before coming into the ground but after 20 minutes they'd want to go to the toilet. That's where the old rolled up Echo would come in handy and people would think they were sweating because they were suddenly nice and warm!

'People handed them over after they were told 'no scarves''

It was even worse at half-time. They used to come out and go towards flagpole corner.

Because the toilet facilities were right down the bottom and couldn't cater for the thousands of people who wanted to use them, they'd line the walls of the actual steps going down and have a pee down the side.

When I was at the back of the Kop by the tea bar I'd try to make sure no-one was doing that in view of the girls who worked there.

I'd get complaints too. Some fella came over once and said "What are you going to do about this?" because it was like a river going down the steps.

He said he wanted them all arrested but it was impossible to arrest all these people because we didn't have sufficient bobbies on duty.

The river would go down and it used to steam. It was totally inadequate the way the system was.

We didn't have the same equipment, in terms of clothing, as we do now.

I remember that we only had thin Macs which didn't provide any warmth at all in those days.

At the time some of the bobbies used to make scarves, which had your collar number in the scarf so no-one would pinch it, and on match day they'd wear them.

But one day the football inspector pointed at the scarves and said 'I don't want to see any of these in the ground today,' which meant he wanted to be able to see our shirts and ties which looked better.

But as time progressed we had sergeants coming from the Kop into the police control room carrying all these red and white scarves.

They'd taken it as 'I don't want to see any scarves inside the ground at all' and had taken them off the fans as they came into the Kop. There were bundles, armfuls of these red and white scarves which they'd taken off people who had handed them over after they'd been told no scarves in here.

They must have took it as 'If you don't give us your scarf you're not coming in' but that's not what he'd meant.

You also used to be able to buy bottles of beer at Liverpool and take them on to the Kop. After drinking a bottle, some of them would be thinking what to do with it and see a copper on the pitch. 'He'll do' and they'd come flying down.

I was on the corner of the Kop for the last game of the 1988/89 season when Arsenal scored in the last minute to take the title.

All the kids, who would sit on the wall at the front of the Kop - and we had to keep an eye on in case they tried to run on to the pitch - were in floods of tears. Grown men and women were crying because of that last minute goal. It was dreadful.

RAY EDWARDS

Gotcha! A police officer catches a young fan in front of the Kop at Anfield and (above) the clean-up operation after the stormy Liverpool v Celtic European Cup Winners' Cup clash of April, 1966

The fences go up: July 1977 and the steel barriers are erected during the summer

The fences come down: Work begins on dismantling the barriers in 1989, in the aftermath of Hillsborough, with tributes scrawled on the Kop wall

The first game I ever policed was St Etienne.

To be down at pitch level that night was quite intimidating. I was a young bobbie and as a junior officer you'd be put down that end because that's where the trouble would be and as young officers we'd be capable of dealing with it.

There were 10,000 Frenchmen at the Anfield Road end singing and shouting that night. It was very intimidating but a tremendous night.

The sergeant at the time always instructed us not to speak to one another when we were down on the pitch.

I was standing there talking with my colleague who had come over to talk to me and the sergeant comes across.

"What have I told you about talking on the pitch?" he said. My colleague replies, "I wasn't talking, Terry was. I was just listening".

So that left me to face the wrath of this sergeant, who is no longer with us, who was a well-known character in football at the time.

There was one game at Everton in the early '90s when, during the game, kids tried to kick a door in on the Bullens Road.

Inspector Swift gets on the PA to say 'This is Merseyside Police. You're on camera and if you do that again you'll be arrested'.

The little ones all ran away but one of them, who was a bit bigger, looks for the camera, drops his pants and moons at us! Maybe not everybody takes notice of us or the cameras.

TERRY McKENNA

I remember well the queues at Lake Street and flagpole corner because it was a common occurrence that people would be locked out, particularly from the Kop.

It was cheap to get in and, apart from the Anfield Road end, the only area with cash turnstiles and also

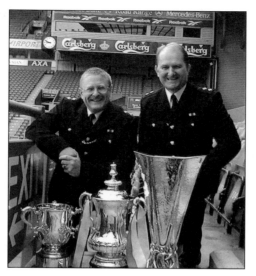

'It was **an art** to see the way the **mounted police** turned the queues and **snaked them** to ease the **pressure**'

the area that was exceptionally popular.

It was an art to see the way the mounted police turned the queues and snaked them to ease the pressure off the front.

No-one likes queuing but people would conform with what you wanted them to do because they wanted to get into the ground. If you asked them to do something they would without a problem.

You'd get the odd moan – 'yer don't know what yer doin'– but you've just got to put up with that. You get that every week but in the main they were good natured.

If there was any trouble we used to have a system where by if somebody was ejected from the stadium the officer would notify the control room and give them a description of where they were ejected from or give their name and address etc.

When we first started this system we had a policewoman who passed a message to the control room that she had just 'ejaculated' a male from the Kop!

I worked the Kop's Last Stand against Norwich and it was a very passionate affair with a lot of flags and a lot of colour.

At the end of the game many people didn't want to leave. They didn't take many souvenirs - there was a concern that they were going to start dismantling the place - but that never happened.

There were a lot of people who didn't want to leave and while we wanted them to go so we could go home, we had to find a balance between clearing the Kop and recognising that it was momentous occasion.

It was a question of dealing with the issue very, very sensitively, which I think we did, but people wanted to stay because it would be their last time there.

TOM KING

'We were on the touchline, a sandwich between the action and the Kop'

I first met the Kop when I was 17 years of age as a young photographer. It was 1966 and I'd never seen anything like it.

As a kid I'd been a Tranmere Rovers fan and spent my sixpence on a Saturday watching them. The first time I was introduced to the Kop I actually had to lie in front of it. It was an unbelievable thing to have had to do.

You'd dress for the Kop. It was one of the few football grounds that you'd actually dress for with protective clothing which was no use whatsoever because it was designed for the elements - not the Kop.

Putting a groundsheet down in front of the Kop then meant that you immediately obliterated any view of the people who had got in there hours before you and were right on the front wall. Their eye-level was grass and they'd be looking along the pitch.

You'd walk round to the Kop in trepidation, lay a groundsheet down and lie flat on your stomach before trying to make yourself disappear into the turf.

Fat photographers didn't stand a chance. I used to feel sorry for them. I also used to feel sorry for photographers who came from foreign countries and sat down instead of lying. They'd only be sat there for a few minutes before they'd be verbally destroyed by the Kop.

So you had to literally try and bury yourself in the ground and that's the most difficult position to try and take photographs because you're lying prostrate.

In those days you'd start off about two feet away from the goalpost. Conversations were regular with the goalkeeper. There were certainly goalkeepers who would talk to us.

John Osborne at West Brom would and Blackpool's Jimmy Armfield, a full-back, would come over and start chatting. It was uncanny being so close to the action.

Unless you got to the Kop pretty quickly you were the end photographer in the line and your elbow would end up on the white line. In really big games at Anfield, all the photographers would want to get down there. We'd all lie down but the angle meant you could only get a maximum of eight photographers.

If you got there too late you were on the touchline and that was the danger zone. Imagine being, and I'm not exaggerating, an inch away from the touchline.

One referee was concerned and stopped a game to move us. But the most difficult thing of all was when people like Steve Heighway and Peter Thompson played. They were wingers who would take the ball to the touchline before crossing.

The momentum of their body and the way they'd wait until the very last second before crossing meant that they couldn't stop. We were a natural cushion for them. When that happened there was a moment of fear. It was like being a sandwich between the action and the crowd. You'd close your eyes and wait for the crunch on your back. It was a regular occurrence. Steve Heighway used to give me nightmares.

European players visiting Anfield were worse. They'd never played in such a tight arena before and they couldn't work out how long it would take them to stop.

They'd go over us and land in the Kop where hands would go up to catch them, except for a Bruges player who ended up landing on my back and knocking me unconscious! I was out cold and had to be brought round by the St John Ambulance people, much to the amusement of the Kop.

Kop life through a lens: Stephen Shakeshaft, pictured closest to the Kop, on match duty at Anfield

They thought it was great fun. 'Yer in for nothing, Mister, we've had to stand here for two hours'. So they'd like you to get soaking wet or whatever.

The Anfield Road end was luxury. On a hot day you could sit in the sun and the crowd were higher up. At half-time you'd walk round to the Kop and on a cold day it was like walking towards a convector heater.

You could feel the heat coming off the thousands of people who were stood together. It was extraordinary.

How comfortable we were depended a lot on the result of the game and what was happening. If there was a bad referee, a goalkeeper they didn't like or a full-back who'd fouled a Liverpool player, the obvious things happened.

You knew what was going to come. There was a shower of stuff. Everything you could imagine but coins mainly. We had old currency in my early days in front of the Kop.

If a fan was really angry he'd throw half a crown, which was a heavy coin and you wouldn't want one of them hitting you on the ear.

The golden rule was never to look at the Kop. If you did you'd take the chance of a coin hitting you in the face. I've also seen meat pies and other things I wouldn't care to mention come flying down. I remember one game when there had been a lot of aggro and I got all the coins together and photographed them. There was enough money there to go and buy a round of drinks which we did after the game.

The other thing was for those who smoked on the Kop, there was nowhere to put their cigarette butts so they'd throw them as well. Many cigarettes landed on my back and burnt through my ▶

▶ coat. You'd hear 'eh Mister, you're on fire'. If you were lucky a policeman would put the fire out with his shoe by standing on your back.

I also saw some awful things like darts being thrown, and I was once fired at with a pellet gun during a European game. Something was twanging off our heads and it turned out to be coming from a hand pistol. I handed a pellet to the police.

I've seen lads being taken out with darts in their faces so there was a side of the Kop that you had to take on board as one of those things you had to put up with.

The good side was the camaraderie. They were so funny. I've laughed so much at some of the natural wit from the Kop. It used to fascinate me how a song would evolve. Something would happen and a player would be singled out. Suddenly, the whole Kop were singing as one, a song that they couldn't possibly have rehearsed.

They all knew the words and some great songs evolved. I remember when they took the pop song 'The Mighty Quinn' and it suddenly became 'The Mighty Emlyn'. They seemed to be able to turn whatever the big pop song was at the time into a song about one of their players.

They'd have special songs for opponent players who they liked, such as Gordon Banks. Players like him would turn round and applaud the Kop although plenty of players would run off quickly because they weren't as popular.

I remember Tommy Smith once wearing white boots for the first time. As soon as he came on the pitch there was a song about it. He was in hysterics because they'd picked up straight away on it.

I don't care what anyone says, I know Rodgers and Hammerstein wrote 'You'll Never Walk Alone' for Carousel but that song has never been more poignant than when it's sung by the Kop on a European night.

Hearing the Kop and Gerry Marsden sing it together make the hairs on the back of your neck stand up. Every time I lay in front of them it was like being in front of a giant stereo.

There were some great characters on there too. I remember the woman with the bell. She'd always be in the same place behind the goal and she'd come in with a fire bell. It'd drive you mad.

Other strange things have happened. I remember losing my shoes once. They didn't have laces on and flicked off as I lay down. I had to persuade this lad to give them me back before I could leave the ground.

Those were the days when the Kop was very full and you'd see people, who had fainted or needed to be taken out, passed down over all the heads. They'd land on top of us too! Once I found a kid had jumped onto the groundsheet next to me and said 'don't tell anyone, Mister, pretend I'm a photographer'.

I told him that I wasn't going to shop him to a policeman but if he was going to lie next to me he'd have to be very quiet. Sure enough, as soon as Liverpool scored, he jumped up in front of me with his arms up. He was pulled out straight away.

As far as my favourite picture goes then there's a photo of Ron Yeats in mid-air I took that I like. He looks like a colossus. He was high in the air and looked like he was jumping over the stands.

Bill Shankly thought the Kop was everything. I was there one day when he was scattering a fan's ashes on the Kop with a family and he came over and asked me what I was doing there. He said I was being intrusive and it was a private moment. I said: "I know, Bill, but the family have asked me to come along and take a picture". I took a picture and that was the only photograph of Bill Shankly scattering ashes on the Kop. No-one had ever seen a picture like that before.

He was very moved because it was one of his lads, one of his supporters who had stood on the Kop.

I remember the day when he stood on the Kop and watched a game. He didn't tell anyone he was going to do it. He was spotted by us. Could you imagine any other manager doing that? The Kop was Shanks' family. That's how he saw them. They were all his sons on that Kop and he was their dad. Everything he did was right. I never once heard one word against Shankly. He was their father. I don't think that could ever happen again.

> 'Once **a kid** jumped onto the **groundsheet** next to me and said 'don't tell anyone, Mister, pretend I'm a photographer''

Taking to the air: Stephen Shakeshaft's remarkable action photo of Ron Yeats at Anfield (below). Left: One of the many colourful characters of the Kop, Dr Fun

The most difficult pictures I've taken in front of the Kop were on the morning after Hillsborough.

I got to Anfield at 7am, after being on Lime Street Station when the fans returned from Sheffield the night before, and they opened the ground up because so many people had arrived to lay flowers.

We walked in single file and I watched lads, sisters, mothers and fathers go to the spot that their brother or sister; son or daughter had stood on the Kop. They'd sit there and tie a little bundle of flowers around the crash barrier.

I felt really intrusive being there with a camera but they were pictures I had to take because they recorded an event that you couldn't believe was happening.

It was so spontaneous. It would only happen at Liverpool.

They had to go to the Kop. It was almost as if they were going to church and had to be there to identify with their son or daughter.

It was the most moving experience.

As I was taking photos, feeling quite intrusive at the time, the Salvation Army had walked in with a band and they played 'Abide With Me'. I found it most tearful.

I've never seen Anfield so quiet. It was like being in a Cathedral.

It wasn't stage-managed, it was all a spontaneous and sincere reaction and took everyone by surprise.

The flowers and scarves were knitted together and it eventually came out to the half-way line.

Liverpool rang me and asked me to come up and take a photograph for them.

I took a picture from the TV gantry to show this carpet. It was filled exactly to the half-way line. It was a tapestry of colour laid by people from around the country. It was incredible.

'I felt **intrusive** being there with **a camera** but they were **pictures** I had to take because they recorded **an event** that you **couldn't believe** was happening. It was so **spontaneous. It would only happen** at Liverpool'

Chain of scarves: Fans come together in an amazing show of unity at Anfield after the Hillsborough disaster. Left: Spelling it out with flowers

'Standing together, united as one in the name of our city'

A terrace of tears: A view from the Kop of the unique carpet of flowers and scarves at Anfield in 1989

On April 21, 1989, I walked the length and breadth of a silent, grieving Kop as the whole of Merseyside, indeed the whole world, mourned the loss of the 96 Liverpool supporters who went to enjoy an FA Cup semi-final at Sheffield Wednesday's Hillsborough Stadium and never returned.

Many of them were proud and loyal Kopites. All of them were dedicated Liverpudlians.

In my role as a Liverpool Echo sports journalist, I had to try and encapsulate and record the agony of those who were desolate in their loss and the reaction of the many hundreds of thousands who were also grieving alongside them as Merseyside desperately tried to come to terms with the tragedy that had rocked us all.

Things happened during those painful days that I will never forget

Of course, we have a memorial to those who lost their lives and even now it is an emotional experience to stand close to that shrine near the Shankly Gates, particularly on a matchday, and watch people amongst the throng, quietly walking past, and touching the ▶

69 🦅

marble bearing the name of a relative or friend and silently vowing never to forget.

The memorial is vital in that respect, immaculately maintained and always bedecked with scarves, cards and flowers.

But for me, the greatest memorial to those who died at Hillsborough had nothing to with anything you could physically reach out and touch.

It had more to do with the way people reacted and how they came together, breaking down all the partisan barriers of football that sometimes border on hatred and even bigotry.

I found it very moving, even symbolic.

Physical barriers had contributed to the crushing within the Leppings Lane end at Sheffield.

Now mental barriers were being cast aside as football fans who previously wouldn't cross the street to hold out the hand of friendship, suddenly travelled the length and breadth of the country to show unity with Liverpool's bereaved.

It was a wonderful thing and it's why I get so very angry when I see bits and pieces of trouble at any games now, especially when it is linked with a Merseyside derby.

Fans nationwide built a monument to camaraderie and respect after the 1989 disaster that none of us should ever forget.

Six days after Hillsborough, this was a report I filed from the Kop which had become a shrine in its own right, a place to be alone with your thoughts, but also a place to be surrounded by friendship and hope for the future. When I read it again, it reminded what a special city this is in which we live . . .

66 *In front of the most famous bank of terracing in English football, the people of Liverpool have been paying their respects to the 95 (it would soon become 96) who died at Hillsborough by turning a football field into a memorial garden.*

And underneath that giant Kop roof, the tributes have taken on a much more personal note.

A thousand and one messages have been written on crush barriers, on the walls and on the concrete terraces themselves, each one of them with its own poignant sentiment.

The Kop has echoed to the sound of silence. The world famous roar that we normally associate with this legendary soccer stronghold has been temporarily muted, but the atmosphere has still been electric.

I walked the length and breadth of the Kop on three successive days this week. The images will live with me forever.

There has been a lot of pain and the tears have flowed freely. But the sight of so many people paying their respects has surely been a comfort to the family and friends of all those who died.

Fans have been visiting Anfield from all corners of Britain. Red has obviously been the dominant colour, but the blue of Everton was in evidence from the word go - and the white of little Tranmere Rovers.

On the Kop itself, scarves representing such diverse soccer centres as Glasgow, Plymouth, Barnsley, Preston, Manchester, London and Sheffield have been hanging side by side - testament to the fact that this disaster has engulfed and united fans everywhere.

There are plans to seat the Kop. When this happens, Anfield will never quite be the same again. But the spirit and togetherness of the fans who inhabit this very special section of Anfield is something that will survive the drawing board changes.

These Echo pages are dedicated to the people who lost their lives at Hillsborough, to the Kopites who will help lead Liverpool into a new era and to every single person who visited Anfield this week to show solidarity with a club in mourning. In their moment of need, Liverpool FC - and families of the bereaved - have taken heart from a famous battle hymn. You'll Never Walk Alone. 99

As I look back on that article now, all these years on, I continue to take heart from the way people reacted and united in grief.

I still believe this was and is the REAL Hillsborough Memorial.

I remember writing: "Liverpool has always looked after its own."

'I walked the length and breadth of the Kop. The images will live with me forever'

The Kop itself was a remarkable focal point, a place to gather, to share memories, to be silent in grief or to let it all flow out.

But something else happened that we should never forget.

Some called it 'The Chain Of Hope.'

The Football Echo page one headline on April 22nd, 1989, declared: 'Link Of Love'.

Final resting place: Ian Snodin, Peter Beardsley and Barry Devonside, father of Hillsborough victim Chris, tie the final scarves in the Chain of Hope

A chain of red and blue scarves began to be tied together, starting at the gates of Goodison Park.

They bridged Walton Lane and ultimately over 4,000 of them would stretch right across Stanley Park, going through the Shankly Gates and right up the The Kop which by now stood like a shrine in front of a carpet of flowers stretching from the goal right out to the centre circle.

I walked the length of that chain, from Everton's famous stadium to the Kop itself, stopping halfway across the park for a pre-arranged interview with a French television crew.

I remember symbolically holding the line of scarves as a circle of people closed in to listen to the broadcast.

I was asked about the disaster itself and whose fault it was and the disgusting allegations that raised their head on the front page of some national newspapers, notably The Sun, under its now infamous headline 'The Truth'. I was proud of the Liverpool Echo at that time.

We highlighted the smear campaign in a powerful page one lead and challenged sections of the national press and the Sheffield Police to produce their evidence. We spoke up powerfully for our city.

Our Old Hall Street base had become the headquarters of the world's press, many of whom descended on Liverpool attracted by some of the scurrilous and totally inaccurate claims that threatened

to outrageously smear Liverpudlians.

I remember one German reporter asking me to take him to "where the hooligans lived". He assumed this would be Toxteth because he had read about the riots that occurred there years earlier.

The fact that these had nothing whatsoever to do with football didn't deflect him from his mission.

It was against this backdrop of mis-information that I spoke to the French TV crew in Stanley Park.

I can't remember the specifics of what I said. The whole day was a blur. But as I spoke up as forcefully as I could for the city of Liverpool, I remember the circle of fans applauding loudly.

They were not applauding me. They were applauding the facts that were crystal clear, that Hillsborough was a mish-mash of blunders by the football authorities, the police who opened the gates to cause the initial surge and the fences that penned people in with no means of escape.

Ironically, it was on similar barriers, in front of the Kop, that the Chain Of Hope reached its journey's end with the last red and blue scarves tied by Liverpool's Peter Beardsley, Everton's Ian Snodin and Barry Devonside whose 18 years old son Chris was killed in Sheffield.

Those fences, along with others all over the country, would soon come down as the lessons of Hillsborough were learned.

The Kop itself would never be quite the same again as the seats came in following Lord Justice Taylor's Report. But it remains the unmistakeable symbol of a football giant, the place where memories live on and future dreams are nurtured.

And seats or no seats, the people are the same. The Kop remains a mighty football institution.

Making his Mark: One of the great nights from the modern era as Mark Walters scores the decisive third goal in a dramatic UEFA Cup comeback against Auxerre in 1991 – a game watched from the Kop by Ashley Neal

'It didn't **occur to me** at the time that I could be the last **Liverpool player** to score at the **Kop end'**

I've always supported Liverpool. I was about six or eight weeks old when we moved to the city because of my dad so I was a big time Liverpool fan from a young age.

I've got pure red blood and I used to stand on the Kop myself.

I was on it for the Auxerre game, which for me is one of the most memorable of them all, and I used to go and stand on it regularly before the club signed me up as a YTS lad.

There's one goal I scored for Liverpool reserves that I will never forget.

We played Nottingham Forest at Anfield shortly before the Kop's last stand and drew the game 2-2.

I scored Liverpool's second goal at the Kop end and it came from a penalty.

Of course, my dad used to take them for Liverpool so there was a little bit of pressure on me.

I remember there was a lad in our team, a Scottish lad, and he was fighting me for the ball.

Luckily enough I was captain of the reserves at the time so I said to him: 'Sod off, I'm having it'.

I stepped up and stuck it into the right corner of the net.

I didn't know it at the time and luckily enough that was the last goal scored in front of the Kop by a Liverpool player.

It didn't occur to me at the time that I could be the last Liverpool player to score at the Kop end.

The Norwich game was after ours and I expected the

Reds to beat them.

In the end they didn't do and Norwich won 1-0 with Jeremy Goss scoring the last league goal in front of the Kop.

What does it mean to me?

I look at it in relation to my dad's career.

He can turn round and say he's got these medals and those medals and that he's Liverpool's most successful footballer ever but I wouldn't swap that for the little piece of history I've got.

That's how much it means to me.

'Every underdog has its

It remains a rare pleasure to attend a match at Liverpool FC. The Kop makes it so.

Long gone are the days when - assured of a prize per season (and a home win per fortnight) - that bank of Scouse passion might have been subject to accusations of only 'singing when they're winning'.

Only the relatively lean times test the strength of a support base. At Anfield, that base is strong and admirable. On Saturday, the colour, the noise and - most of all - the appreciation of footballing endeavour were magnificently vivid. Liverpool, meanwhile, lost 1-0 to the hot relegation favourites.

It is awkward when discussing the Kop - as it is with the Church - to know whether one is referring to a building or those who congregate in it.

In fact, neither would be anything without the other - a few thousand bucket-seats on a sloped expanse of concrete and a few thousand football followers with nowhere to gather - but it is the people who give life to the building. What a necessary service those people did for the game last weekend.

By 2.30pm the Kop was filling up. Scarves head-high and horizontally-taut, the Kop's first rendition of 'You'll Never Walk Alone' echoed with audibly genuine 'hope in their hearts'.

It drew applause from the Watford fans and created a momentum of support that lasted for much of the game.

Nobody booed when the Watford team-sheet was read out; everybody clapped when the Watford goalkeeper ran towards them for the start of the second half.

Then at the end -

Looking after their own: Kopites were regularly passed over other Kopites' heads if the situation demanded it

and here was the highlight for anyone who clings anachronistically on to ideals of mutual respect, sportsmanship or simple decency - they stayed behind to applaud their victorious visitors.

Of course they are not perfect - what several-thousand-strong mass of humanity is?

Acknowledgement is duly made of very noticeable recent impatience among some Kopites which flies in the face of their fabled unconditional support.

Furthermore, there are, no doubt, some who would seek to recount less happy experiences of Anfield, and many more who believe their own club's support to be comparably good.

However, what happened at the weekend deserves to be held up as an example. It was sufficiently good and sufficiently rare to draw an affectionate word from the visiting manager.

Graham Taylor was right when he said: "In these days of all the tension, hype and pressure of the modern game, it was good to hear fans do that. I know my players were impressed and will remember it. It is to those fans' credit that they can do that. They weren't saying we were better than their players, but they appreciated how we had played".

I spoke on the subject to Ian St John who, having run out at Anfield more often and longer ago than he would probably prefer to recall, still rarely misses a match.

He described such conduct as 'standard'. His was one of the early names to be singled out for chanting by the Kop. Like 'Dal-glish' in

day in front of the **Kop'**

later years, he was fortunate that his two syllables offered just the right emphasis to follow a rhythmic handclap.

That level of support added playing inches to a small man and the ethos of the Anfield crowd remains something of which he is proud.

"If an underdog comes up and plays the right way . . . with endeavour and organisation and without kicking lumps out of Liverpool, the crowd will appreciate that and they'll be applauded.

"I recall a famous Cup tie against Swansea in the early '60s when we absolutely murdered them. But it was one of those games in which their goalkeeper made about 25 brilliant saves.

"I got concussed and was blacking out but, in those days, they made you play on and, by the end, I think I was probably kicking the wrong way.

"It was terrible . . . but the Kop were great to them. At Liverpool, that's standard. It's tradition".

That tradition might have gone into decline after the installation of seats - (not, of course, that anyone at Liverpool objected to that) - and St John, like all devotees of the club, recalls the terraced Kop's "unique swaying and singing. After all, at rock concerts they stand. You do it better standing up".

But, through the dark days of the trauma which necessitated those seats, the tradition has survived and the perspective has sharpened.

On the Kop, they love Liverpool but they understand that, without an opponent, there isn't a game.

Without Watford and Swansea, and even Everton and Manchester United, Liverpool is a pretty pointless entity.

Pointless is precisely what Saturday became for Liverpool. Happily, the Kop offered that pointlessness some meaning.

From THE INDEPENDENT newspaper, August 1999

A very big thank you to Liverpool fans. I know I speak for all 7,000 Bristol City supporters in saying how moved and gratified we were at the fabulous reception we received at the finish of the game on January 25th (1994). We were amazed and totally thrilled. Thank you again.

G PRITCHARD

I am a Bristol City supporter and was at Anfield. The best moment that night wasn't when we scored or even when the final whistle went. For me, the lasting memory will be of the reception the visiting players received after the game from the Kop. I've often heard that Liverpool fans were the best in the country - now I know it's true.

JAMES McANDREW

I was fortunate to be one of the visiting fans from Bristol at Anfield. My lasting memory of the occasion was the magnificent ovation the Kop gave at the end. It was truly an emotional moment and the gesture will always live in my memory. There is no need to look beyond the Kop as the Sports Personalities of the Year. Thanks for the memory.

D FERRAR
(All Bristol City fans at Anfield after their FA Cup win at Anfield in January, 1994)

'It was truly emotional. There is no need to look beyond the Kop as the Sports Personalities of the Year'

One of my best memories was the 2-1 FA Cup quarter-final win at Anfield in 1995.

It wasn't just playing and scoring but walking off the pitch to a standing ovation from the Kop.

TEDDY SHERINGHAM
Former Tottenham and England striker

From the moment Shankly arrived there's been only one way - up. And this endless success was mirrored in that amazing relationship with the Kop.

When he was at Anfield he was the city of Liverpool's answer to vandalism and hooliganism because the kids came to see Liverpool.

They came to see those red shirts and Shankly was their man, their hero, their football God.

He belongs to the Kop. He's one of them. If he hadn't managed Liverpool I'm sure he'd have been on the Kop dressed in red, singing and chanting 'Liverpool, Liverpool'.

JOE MERCER OBE
Ex-Everton and Arsenal player, ex-Man City and Aston Villa manager

We had Shankly and the Kop at Liverpool and the partnership made you feel you could do anything.

We were brainwashed into thinking we could win everything. It was a great feeling.

PETER THOMPSON
Former Liverpool player

When our kid and I were children, Dad used to take us to Liverpool's and Everton's matches.

I'll never forget our first visit to Anfield, complete with scarves, overcoats, vacuum flasks - the lot.

Many years later when 'Thank U Very Much' was becoming a British hit, we were asked to make a promo film for the United States. Our director, Jim Goddard, wanted to use the Royal angle and include a film of the Kop singing the last two lines . . . 'thank you very much for our gracious TEAM' instead of Queen. (Geddit?)

Roger McGough was elsewhere on the day so just John Gorman (in loud check suit) and I (with long hair) presented ourselves at the packed ground on match day with very mixed feelings. What if they didn't like it? What if they didn't know it?

Our worst feelings were almost realised in front of that massive Kop audience when the record didn't play on cue. But we soon knew they were on our side - they roared together as one voice: 'Oh where d'ya get dat sewt? Oh where d'ya get dat sewt? Oh where d'ya get dat sewt?' . . . 'Getcher hur cut . . . getcher hur cut'.

Then the song came on and they sang it better than the record - with the bonus of a massive sea of red and white scarves swaying in time.

MIKE McCARTNEY
The Scaffold

I was making a recording of the crowd during a European match. The wit was pouring off the Kop in torrents and I was semi-conducting them. It was very emotional and when they finished I applauded them.

I was putting my recording gear away, still with tears in my eyes, when this little urchin on the wall called "Eh, Mister, come 'ere".

Thinking perhaps he wanted my autograph I went over to him. "Yes, son?" I beamed.

He looked me straight in the eye and said: "Why don't yer gerroff, yer short-arsed git!"

STUART HALL
Commentator and journalist

> '**I went over to him. 'Yes, son' I beamed. He looked me straight in the eye and said: "Why don't yer gerroff, yer short-arsed git!"'**

Manchester City were winning 2-1 with six minutes to go at Anfield and I took a corner at the Kop end. They gave me some stick so I lowered my shorts. Minutes later they had gone 3-2 ahead through Roger Hunt and Ian St John and the Kop chanted: "Show us your backside, Summerbee". At least it sounded something like that! They were great fans though and fair to all visiting players who earned their respect.

MIKE SUMMERBEE
Former Manchester City player

We all live in a red and white Kop: Kopites have been known to do all sorts of things for the love of their team. Top: A fan decked out in colours. Above: It's not tin hats but bicycle helmets for this '70s fan. Left: This Kopite grew a red rose which he named after the Spion Kop!

'The Kop threw me a raw chop and shouted: Here's your dinner!'

The Kop has meant everything to me down the years. As a young lad I used to stand on that famous bank of terracing, following in the footsteps of my dad.

Later I would play in front of the Kop hundreds of times, first as one of Bill Shankly's young brigade and later as a seasoned pro under Bob Paisley.

I suppose my first memories of the Kop are linked with waiting outside the ground at three-quarter time with what seemed like an army of people, men and boys, who used to slip in for a taste of the action when the gates opened for the early leavers.

I could never understand why anyone would want to go home before the final whistle.

Here we were, Liverpudlians on the outside, all desperately wanting to be on the inside.

Many boys who couldn't afford to pay full whack to get in from the start gained their first taste of big time football by going in at three-quarter time.

It was common practice and nobody stopped you.

The logic was simple. Once you had experienced life on the Kop, you would be hooked for life.

Of course, you didn't just go to watch the first team. I can remember going to watch the reserves.

It wasn't quite as crowded in the Kop and you could find your feet without being lifted off them as was the case in first team games when the fans surged forward.

You'd always try and get in front of a crush barrier, not behind one, but most people had their own spec, even though it was obviously a massive standing terrace with no reserved places.

Somehow people still managed to stand on exactly the same spot every week.

It was an education in there and you always came away with a smile on your face.

I remember when we had some quite chunky individuals playing down the left.

I remember this old Scouser declaring: "What do you see when you look down our left hand side? Ronnie Moran, Phil Ferns, Johnny Morrissey. When they're close together, it's like watching one giant backside powering forward like a ten ton truck!"

What an image to lock in your mind. The Kop was full of jokers.

When I signed for Liverpool, I saw it from the other side.

I used to regularly have a chat with people in the Kop when the ball went dead. You got to know many of the faces in the crowd.

I can remember playing in a rough house of a game against Leeds, par for the course against them.

After one challenge, Terry Yorath came down heavily on top of me over by the corner flag on the Kemlyn Road side.

I pushed him off and was just about to crack him when I felt something hit me on the shoulder.

I looked down and there was a raw pork chop beside me on the pitch, thrown from the Kop.

This voice shouted: "Here's your dinner Smithy, leave him alone!"

I couldn't help but laugh. Another time, we were playing Coventry City. They had a lanky Scottish winger called Tommy Hutchison.

He was having a nightmare and during a break in the play I was sitting on the wall talking to the fans in the Kop and taking the p*** out of him.

He was about to go to the World Cup with Scotland and I was taking every opportunity to wind him ▶

Iron man: No-one epitomised the Shankly spirit more than Tommy Smith, in action in front of the Kop (above)

Left: At Anfield for the Kop's Last Stand in 1994 with Ian Callaghan, Billy Liddell and Albert Stubbins

▶ up. Hutchison was going mad and it didn't help when we got a penalty and Alec Lindsay rolled it into the corner.

"Lucky *******", shouted the Coventry winger. I said: "Shut up you moaning Scottish ****".

This was all going on in the heat of battle. He suddenly said: "I'll tell you what Smithy, let's see who's the best. I'll race you to the halfway line. Twenty quid I beat you hands down".

I wasn't the fastest of defenders. I used other tactics to hold my own.

"Okay, lad," I said. "I'll take your bet if you double it up to take mine. After we've had the race, we'll have a fight. I know who'll be going home with the money!"

The Kop was always quick to pick up on any banter between the players. When that roar went up it made the hairs stand up on the back of your neck. I was so proud when I later became Liverpool captain and would lead the team out on to the pitch.

The Kop would be singing "You'll Never Walk Alone".

It was so inspirational. Having been a Kopite myself, it made it extra special when they roared your name.

That bank of terracing was sacred ground. Once you became a Kopite, you didn't go anywhere else. You were part of a club within the club.

In the Sixties, Liverpool was the centre of the universe. The Beatles were just starting out and Merseyside was booming at that time.

The Kop invented all these songs and chants that had no equal in football.

For me, it's where it all began. The whole world copied the Kop, but there was only one genuine article.

Leeds goalkeeper Gary Sprake threw the ball straight into his own net as he tried to launch it clear. The Kop were immediately singing 'Careless Hands' from the Des O'Connor hit of the day.

You'd go to take a throw-in and there were always hundreds of people shouting advice and telling you what do.

It was like having 25,000 coaches at one end of the ground, all very knowledgeable in their own right.

Liverpudlians know their football, no doubt about that.

The humour was never very far away.

I remember Joe Corrigan, the current goalkeeping coach, going in goal at half time at the Kop end for one of those penalty competitions.

Joe, a good keeper during his days with Manchester City, put on a bit of beef when he stopped playing. One penalty was stuck in the bottom corner and he dived and missed it.

Someone shouted: "You would have got that Joe, if it had been a pie".

Typical Kop humour!

When you look at footage of the standing Kop at its peak, it's an awesome sight.

Of course, Bill Shankly was the undisputed King of the Kop. He loved them and they loved him.

> **'The first thing they ask is 'What was it like to play for Liverpool?' The second is 'What was it like to play in front of the Kop?"**

Shanks always wanted to be one of them. He actually went in the Kop at the end of his career on one occasion.

The thing I remember was one of those famous days when we paraded another trophy around the pitch.

Kopites were throwing their red scarves on to the track for us to pick up.

Shanks already had a couple around his neck. A policeman kicked one aside and the boss was furious.

He let the copper know in no uncertain terms.

Shanks demanded that the fans were treated with the utmost respect.

The Kop was pure gold as far as he was concerned and it was the same for me. I've been lucky enough to travel all over the world. You can be thousands of miles away and walking down the street and someone will suddenly recognise you.

The first thing they ask is: "What was it like to play for Liverpool FC?" The second thing they ask is: "What was it like to play in front of the Kop?"

It's an easy answer for me. 'Absolutely wonderful'.

The Kop was as much a part of Liverpool's success as the team.

Just like my old boss Shanks, I hold them in the highest regard.

'The noise frightened me'

The Kop were always fantastic to me. In all honesty I think I was a sort of quiet hero to them whereas others were vocal heroes.

When I came out on to the pitch, and they were chanting people's names, they never chanted my name. There was a mutual respect there though and they were great to play in front of.

Funnily enough one of the games that showed me what the Kop was all about came when we got beaten at home by Birmingham. It was January '78 and we were 3-0 down. Trevor Francis was a scorer. Anyway, we were 3-0 down and all of a sudden the Kop went ballistic.

We got two back in the last 18 minutes or so and I tell you what, if the game had gone on we'd have won by six in the end. I'm not kidding you, it was unbelievable. That was the only real time when the Kop of the late '70s and early '80s was like the Kop of the mid '60s. If you could imagine playing in front of that . . . it wasn't a goal start it was a two goal start. The crescendo of noise was unbelievable. I remember playing in my first derby match at Anfield in September '77. When I went on that pitch, I tell you what, I couldn't hear myself think.

The noise levels frightened me. I was on the pitch and I thought to myself 'Christ, what's this?'. You go to a Liverpool v Everton match now and they're still vocal but its nothing like it was. As I said, the Kop of the late '70s and early '80s never quite matched the Kop of the mid '60s.

People talk about complacency but it wasn't just the Kop that was complacent but the crowd in general. When people talk about Liverpool supporters, and talk about their vocal support, then in the main they talk about the Kop. That's true but I think there was a general malaise in the Liverpool supporters in the 1980s. They just won too much. We'd be coming off after winning 2-0 or 3-0 and they were groaning.

There was a lot of talk in 2003-2004 about the Liverpool crowd's reaction to what they saw as negative tactics in trying to kill a game off. I remember playing and we'd be 2-0 up and the bench are shouting 'give it back to the keeper'. We'd keep hold of it across the back four and the first time we did it they'd start counting the passes or whatever.

The second time we'd do it you'd start to hear the grunts, the groans and the dismay. They were always fantastic to me though and my testimonial at Anfield was extra special. We'd just been beaten in the FA Cup Final by Wimbledon but 33,000 turned up. It was frightening. There was a great atmosphere. Rushie had come back to play and Kenny played with him.

It was like going back into the halcyon days with the Rush and Dalglish partnership. Bobby Robson was unbelievable. He brought his England team who were going to Euro '88 and he played a strong side because he wanted a run-out for them. It finished 3-2 and it was a great game. The crowd loved it.

Memorable day: The Kop enjoyed Liverpool beating England in Alan Hansen's testimonial

'It was the proudest moment of my life in football, for sure'

The Kop's Last Stand was a special day to say the least. I've put that day down as the proudest moment of my footballing career, to be honest, because it was such a huge event and such a huge day.

The whole world knows about the Kop end at Anfield. Norwich were in tremendous form going into the game. We'd had a brilliant season but we knew going to Liverpool on that day was going to be hard for us.

We thought with all the razzmatazz and all the hype it's going to be a tough game because they're going to be up for it in a massive way. We were all chatting about it before the game and we all thought Rushie was going to be the last guy who'd score in front of the standing Kop.

He deserved to be the guy who'd score that goal at that end and be remembered forever and rightly so, because of his services to the club and being the world class goalscorer that he was.

Unbelievably, I popped up from nowhere and suddenly it was my name that was down on the list as the last guy to score at the Kop end. It was the proudest moment of my life in football for sure.

I was quite fortunate that the good goals I scored were on the box.

The Liverpool game was highlighted heavily on TV, the Bayern Munich games were live on TV and I was lucky enough to score twice against them and a goal I scored at Leeds won me the Match of the Day goal of the month award.

The best goal I've ever scored was at Leeds. No doubt. But the goal at Anfield was my proudest.

It was just one of those things where I tried my best to shoot and score.

I just tried to hit the target.

I'd had one or two goals that season that had flown in and I was in a good vein of form.

I was at the top of my game. It was the fittest I'd ever been, the strongest I'd ever been and I was confident in gambling and hitting things.

Normally I'd take a touch and pass it on but during that spell I was just hitting them.

A corner was headed out to me and I chested it down. It took a bounce and I just struck through the ball and hit the target.

It could have flown into the Kop but luckily for me I think David James was just standing there as it flew in.

I've got two pictures at home on my wall from that day.

One is of that particular strike. The picture is taken from behind me as I've hit the ball and you can see Neil Ruddock closing me down and David James watching it fly past him.

I've also got a picture of me celebrating, running away with my arms in the air. Again, another compliment to the Liverpool fans really, there are hundreds of people in the Kop end, with their arms outstretched, clapping.

They were just clapping me and I remember that.

They just clapped the goal because they thought 'well played, good goal'.

That's the type of fans Liverpool have got.

The atmosphere was electric. It really, really was special.

We got introduced to Gerry Marsden before the game. The lads realised then what a big game,

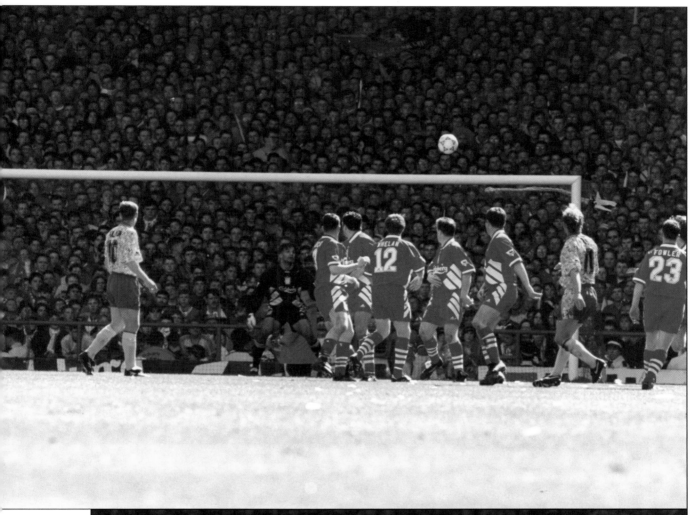

Going, going, Goss: Jeremy Goss looks on as his shot heads into the Kop end net

Kop that: The Norwich players celebrate an historic goal

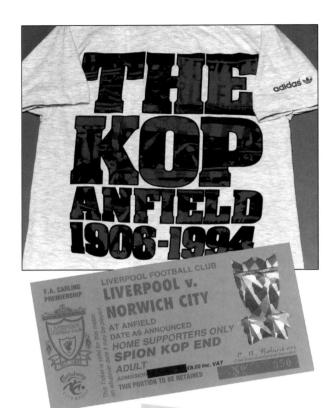

End of an era: Souvenirs from a famous day – a ticket stub, specially designed T-shirt and a Liverpool Echo supplement

'The **fans** are the best in the **country**, for me. They really do **appreciate** good teams, good players and good **goals**'

▶ what a monster game it was.

It was also a lovely game to be involved in.

We were the last team to go to Anfield and play in front of the standing Kop and it was something special for us all.

The atmosphere was simply electric and one of expectation too: 'Who was going to be the last guy to score in front of the Kop?'

I'm sure they were begging for it to be Rushie.

My goal came in the first half but I never gave it a thought that no-one else would score.

During the game all I knew was that we were winning 1-0 and I felt great.

We were playing well and our objective was to win the game. We were out to do a job and I know it was a party atmosphere for Liverpool but we weren't just going to roll over and get beaten.

It was only when the final whistle blew I thought about it.

All the Norwich City fans were chanting my name. I was walking over to them and I thought 'my God'.

There was then a five minute spell where I just literally stood there taking it all in before we all went down to the Kop end and applauded them.

It was an unbelievable scene, one that is hard to describe today.

Everyone had their scarves and their flags up and we were all clapping the Kop end.

I'm sure for some of the Liverpool players, like Ian Rush, it would have been quite emotional.

The Kop was never to be seen again.

I got hundreds of letters after that game from Scousers who said 'It hurts me to say this but well done.

'I wanted to congratulate you on being the last guy . . . you're going to go down in history as the last guy to score at the Kop end'.

I was taken aback by it and always have been about playing against Liverpool at Anfield.

It was a brilliant place to go.

The fans there are the best in the country, for me. They really do appreciate good teams, good players and good goals.

I was lucky enough to be clapped and applauded and receive lots of letters from them.

They are brilliant memories and it was a very, very special moment in my life.

The Last Stand:
The fans say goodbye to the standing Kop in style during the Norwich game

Left: Robbie Fowler flies the flag after the 1-0 defeat

The party's over: A last poignant look out from the famous old terrace after its last stand in 1994

'Final goodbyes to a

The Saturday night was drawing to its unyielding close. I sat at the foot of our stairs, head slightly bowed, hands clasped consolingly down between my knees.

I was alone save for our dog. Albie, who lay prostrate alongside the front door several feet away.

His skewed, doleful eyes peered up towards me, meeting my own gaze with somewhat bemused resignation. He was aware something was amiss if not sure exactly what.

Certainly, he could tell a late night walk wasn't on the immediate agenda. He was right, too.

Scarcely pausing for breath, I began delivering my entire repertoire of Liverpool songs to our empty house and a by now disconsolate Albie who wanted none of it, having just had confirmed his worst fears concerning his walk, prompting him to slink off dejectedly towards the back kitchen.

Of course, both Albie and the house had heard those same songs resonate around every nook and cranny countless times before.

Like the other members of the household they had grown accustomed down the years to my lusty exaltations of the men in red.

tried and trusted **friend'**

It was different this time, though. This time, the gusto that usually accompanied each exaltation was simply not there.

Instead, were just fleeting jagged remnants of defiance, almost as if I were making token efforts to claw back some redress for the emotions I was feeling.

A few lines into You'll Never Walk Alone and the grim realisation of the day's events gripped me even tighter. Occasional tears welled up and spilled. Not a flood. No histrionics.

But enough, nevertheless, to make our peerless anthem even more challenging to complete solo than usual, cramping my delivery and demanding

intermittent droplets be wiped away.

Sure, the preceding skinful at the Thirlmere may not have helped on the waterworks front. However, it was not alcohol that was fuelling my sadness that evening. Several hours earlier I had bade farewell to a major chunk of my life.

The curtain had been drawn over the Anfield Spion Kop and like many thousands of others my heart was aching.

After forty-odd years, final goodbyes to a tried and trusted friend are no easy matter.

Even an equally forlorn Albie could, I'm sure, sense that.

Stay behind: Fans refuse to leave the Kop after the 'Last Stand' in 1994

Silent tribute: The Kop's famous flagpole at half mast on a wet day in 1981 – marking the death of the legendary Bill Shankly

'That draw was earned by the Kop, by its deafening reminder to the players of just what Liverpool FC means to the fans'

'I do miss the old Kop.
It was, as Shankly said,
like a 12th man'

I'm going to pick a match from Souness' disastrous time in charge. It was an evening game against Man Utd and it was to be the last time we played them in front of a standing Kop.

I went with Chris Eccleston and his girlfriend. At the time Chris was famous for two things: he was starring in Cracker and he was a lifelong Man Utd fan.

Not a chance of him going in the Kop. We got three seats in the Centenary Stand.

Within minutes Man Utd were three nil up and Chris and his girlfriend were grinning from ear to ear.

Then the Kop got to work. A crescendo of noise.

I was only twenty yards away and I was getting it full blast.

It was awe inspiring and even that crap team that Graeme had sent out responded to it.

Even Nigel Clough, for God's sake, decided to get stuck in.

By half time it was 2-3. At the final whistle it was 3-3. We had fielded a lousy team, given the Mancs a three goal start, and still ended up with an honourable draw.

Believe me, that draw had little to do with that Liverpool team.

Even less to do with the manager.

That draw was earned by the Kop, by its deafening reminder to the players of just what Liverpool FC means to its fans.

After the match Alex Ferguson said of the Kop, "It's a shame that such wonderful support is going to disappear."

He was right. In the competitions that really matter, Liverpool FC has achieved nothing since the Kop went all seater.

That's not to say that Kopites should stand. Far from it. Better a hundred years in the football wilderness than another 96 dead.

But I do miss the old Kop. It was, as Shankly said, a twelfth man.

Without it these days, we're down to eleven.

'The Kop had all the colour of a **matchday** but no people. It was weird'

It's the queuing I remember. Queuing in an eerie silence I had never heard before.

I can't remember exactly where we joined the queue. Somewhere alongside the railings next to Stanley Park car park, I think.

I just remember thinking how I'd never seen so many people queue at the same time and make so little noise.

I'd only ever been to Anfield before on match days. It was always noisy outside the ground.

The hubub of the crowd. The anticipation of the game. The souvenir sellers shouting 'get yer hats, caps, scarves or yer t-shirts'.

But this was different. Very different. It brought home to me exactly what had happened at Hillsborough.

I was 11 at the time. I wasn't at Hillsborough on April 15, 1989.

I wasn't allowed to go to away matches. Too young.

In any case, my dad was a Blue so there'd probably have been more chance of me being taken to Villa Park that afternoon if we'd gone to a cup semi-final.

We didn't. Our family went to buy a new washing machine instead.

So I spent the afternoon watching the tragedy unfold on 20 tellys in the St Helens branch of Currys.

The magnitude of what was happening didn't initially sink in.

At first I remember being disappointed that the game had been called off and there wouldn't be any highlights on TV that night.

Then, as talk of a death toll emerged, that disappointment gave way to the realisation that Liverpool fans had died.

The following morning I turned up to play for my Sunday League Under-12s side, Parr & Hardshaw.

All the talk was about Hillsborough. The older brother of one of the lads in our team had gone to the game.

He was okay. I can't say for sure but I think he'd been sat in the upper-tier of the Leppings Lane end. I remember feeling glad he was alright and that now I actually knew someone who'd been there.

We held a minute's silence before the game.

The silence of people queuing outside Anfield to pay their respects lasted a lot longer.

It was hours before we got into the ground.

As we'd queued I'd thought to myself that for the first time I'd actually get to walk on the Anfield pitch and stand in front of the Kop.

That was an exciting prospect.

I'm sure I was not the only 12-year-old in that queue who was thinking along those lines.

My excitement immediately disappeared when I entered the ground.

Seeing Anfield's pitch and the Kop covered in flowers on the telly was one thing, seeing it with my own two eyes was another. It took my breath away.

This wasn't Anfield. Not the Anfield I'd been to before. This was a shrine. A shrine of the like I'd never seen before and have never seen since.

My mum laid flowers on the pitch that was now covered with floral tributes beyond the Kop end penalty box.

My brother and I had taken our treasured Liverpool

A sea of flowers and scarves: The remarkable outpouring of emotion and colour as Anfield paid tribute to the Hillsborough victims, captured in a photo taken from the Anfield TV gantry by Stephen Shakeshaft

scarves with us.

We'd only got those scarves quite recently. They were our 'best scarves'. Much thicker, warmer and redder than our originals.

I don't know about our Andy but I remember being reluctant to part with mine at first.

It was only when we'd walked back down the touchline towards the Annie Road end that I decided to leave it there.

I gave that scarf to a steward who tied it to the side-netting on the goal down that end.

By then I'd only ever sat in the Annie Road end to watch Liverpool. It seemed somehow appropriate that my scarf ended up down there.

As we left the ground via the away terracing in the corner of the Kemlyn Road stand I remember looking back towards the Kop.

It had all the colour of a matchday but none of the people. Wierd.

It's an eerie image I'll never forget.

Anfield shrine: The now famous and haunting image as a sea of scarves and flowers provides a fitting tribute to the victims of the Hillsborough disaster

Jack Anderson (62)

Colin Mark Ashcroft (19)

James Gary Aspinall (18)

Kester Roger Marcus Ball (16)

Gerard Baron Snr (67)

Simon Bell (17)

Barry Bennett (26)

David John Benson (22)

David William Birtle (22)

Tony Bland (22)

Paul David Brady (21)

Andrew Mark Brookes (26)

Carl Brown (18)

Steven Brown (25)

Henry Thomas Burke (47)

Peter Andrew Burkett (24)

Paul William Carlile (19)

Raymond Thomas Chapman (50)

Gary Christopher Church (19)

Joseph Clark 'oey (29)

Paul Clark (18)

Gary Collins (22)

Stephen Paul Copoc (20)

Tracey Elizabeth Cox (23)

James Philip Delaney (19)

Christopher Barry Devonside (18)

Chris Edwards (29)

Vincent Michael Fitzsimmons (34)

Steve Fox (21)

Jon-Paul Gilhooley (10)

Barry Glover (27)

Ian Thomas Glover (20)

Derrick George Godwin (24)

Roy Hamilton (34)

Philip Hammond (14)

Eric Hankin (33)

Gary Harrison (27)

Stephen Francis Harrison (31)

Peter Andrew Harrison (15)

Dave Hawley (39)

James Robert 'Jimmy' Hennessy (29)

Paul Anthony Hewitson (26)

Carl Hewitt (17)

Nick Hewitt (16)

Sarah Louise Hicks (19)

Victoria Jane Hicks (15)

Gordon Horn 'Goffer' (20)

Arthur Horrocks (41)

Thomas Howard (39)

Tommy Anthony Howard (14)

Eric George Hughes (42)

Alan Johnston (29)

Christine Anne Jones (27)

Gary Philip Jones (18)

Richard Jones Bsc (25)

Nicholas Peter Joynes (27)

Anthony P Kelly (29)

Michael Kelly (38)

Carl David Lewis (18)

David William Mather (19)

Brian Christopher Matthews (38)

Francis Joseph McAllister (27)

John McBrien (18)

Marian Hazel McCabe (21)

Joe McCarthy (21)

Peter McDonnell (21)

Alan McGlone 'Gloney' (28)

Keith McGrath (17)

Paul Brian Murray (14)

Lee Nicol (14)

Stephen Francis O'Neill (17)

Jonathon Owens (18)

William Roy Pemberton (23)

Carl Rimmer (21)

Dave Rimmer (38)

Graham John Roberts HND (24)

Steven Robinson (17)

Henry Charles Rogers (17)

Andrew Sefton (23)

Inger Shah (38)

Paula Ann Smith (26)

Adam Edward Spearritt (14)

Philip John Steele (15)

David Leonard Thomas (23)

Pat Thompson (35)

Peter Reuben Thompson (30)

Stuart Thompson (17)

Peter F Tootle (21)

Christopher James Traynor (26)

Martin Kevin Traynor (16)

Kevin Tyrrell (15)

Colin Wafer (19)

Ian 'Ronnie' Whelan (19)

Mr. Martin Kenneth Wild (29)

Kevin Daniel Williams (15)

Graham John Wright (17)

'All my life I've gone out and people have asked: 'Where's your handbag?''

Hey there, Gordon West: Everton's keeper can't believe what's happened as the ball nestles in the net during a derby in 1968

I remember my first derby game and I didn't know about the rivalry between the two clubs.

So I went down and stood in front of the Kop and they were all sticking two fingers up at me, poking and swearing, all aimed at me.

I just couldn't believe anybody could be like that.

Don't forget, I was only a kid. I was only 19 and it was an eye-opener.

The year after I learnt and thought I would sort the

Liverpool fans out so I started blowing them kisses and showing them a bit of bottom. I thought it was really funny.

The following year, that's when I got the handbag. It ruined my life!

You ask anybody in Liverpool about Gordon West and they will mention Sandy Brown's own goal and the handbag - and I've played for England. It is unbelievable.

All my life I have gone out and had a pint and I have had people asking 'Where's your handbag?'

Kop that! The now famous incident from September, 1967, as a Liverpool supporter hands Everton keeper Gordon West a handbag with the name 'Honey West' written on it

I never ever went to Anfield and got absolutely slaughtered so I always enjoyed playing in front of the Kop.

When you're a kid, you look in awe at the Kop, then when you're a goalkeeper and you look at the reception every goalkeeper gets there, you look forward to the day you play in front of it.

To be fair, it didn't disappoint me. Playing in front of the Kop was really good and I've got a lot of respect for those people who stood on it.

Sometimes I'd hear things they were shouting at me but it was never stupid. It was always good-natured.

I didn't mind that and I always looked forward to playing at Anfield because I thought it was a decent ground. There was always a good atmosphere and if you're any sort of footballer you always wanted to play in front of the Kop.

To be honest I don't remember my first game there. I was young and I was stupid so I never even thought about what type of reception I'd get as Everton's goalkeeper at Anfield. I just enjoyed playing there and it became a ground I looked forward to going to, even though they were our main enemies.

One game that sticks out in my mind came in the derby after somebody had thrown bananas at John Barnes. When we played at Anfield the next time someone on the Kop kept throwing leeks at me. They didn't reach the goal though. They were crap throwers! I thought it was quite funny to be fair and there was no harm in it.

'They threw leeks

I think the Kop changed though with the introduction of more foreign goalkeepers. I don't know what it was - maybe they liked British goalkeepers better - but it changed. I have to say that I also think they were crippled by Heysel and it wasn't their fault. Others were at fault because whoever went there should have said this ground ain't good enough.

Unfortunately, Liverpool have carried that burden and I think it destroyed the Kop. There was never any trouble on the Kop. I know what happened at Hillsborough but that wasn't trouble or the ground. That was a series of events.

They had to put seats in and I don't think that was right. They should have left it as it was. For me they should have left it as the Kop and I still think the people would have been quite happy standing there.

The Kop was unique, like the people in the city.

The way Liverpool and Everton fans are ▶

Saving the best: The Kop watches anxiously as Bruce Grobbelaar stretches athletically to keep out an Everton effort during the '80s

at me – I just **laughed!'**

Speedie delivery: Neville Southall and Dave Watson on the receiving end of a famous David Speedie goal in the 1991 Mersey derby at Anfield, celebrated by Glenn Hysen

> is different to anywhere else in the country. If you play for Everton or Liverpool and play Man United, or get to a final, then most will stick up for you.

The times when we came back to the city after we'd won stuff, Liverpool fans were always out cheering. I've looked at every other derby I've ever seen and that's why ours is unique.

The people are unique. If Everton are playing Man United I think Liverpool supporters want Everton to win. The people are proud of the city and they all stick together. There's the Kop and the Gwladys Street and everybody knows about them.

The Kop was world famous. Obviously they won more than us so I suppose that's why the Kop became more famous than the Gwladys Street. It's like having a brother. If you play against each other you want to beat s**t out of each other and you want to win all the time.

But if it comes down to it and someone attacks Liverpool you don't hear 'well I'm a Red or I'm a Blue, blah, blah, blah,' you hear 'we're from Liverpool'. That's why the fans would stand together at derby games because at the end of the day they've got one thing in common, they're from the same city and they're proud of it. That comes across wherever you go.

They will stand together and fight anybody who has a bad word to say about them but will also fight like s**t amongst themselves.

You go into any Liverpool pub when there's been a Liverpool v Everton game and it's all 'you lost Saturday' or whatever. I'll tell you what though, you try and attack them - and I've seen people do it - and say something bad about the city and they'll put you in your place.

They won't have it and that's the best thing about the city and the two clubs for me. You don't get that in Manchester or anywhere else. They'll fight their corner but they won't fight anybody else's.

In Liverpool they'll fight their corner and either the Blue or Red corner as well because it's their city. The hardcore of Liverpool fans, and the same goes for Everton, are from Liverpool and they created the two best ends of grounds I have ever played in front of. Those two ends were unique and the noise was always deafening, even if the games weren't fantastic.

NEVILLE SOUTHALL

I always regarded it as the greatest honour in football. If you got on with them, they got on with you. I probably got more support from the Kop than I ever did at The Hawthorns.

I remember in one match there was a break in play because someone was injured.

I was waiting to take a goal kick so I walked back and sat on the wall in front of the Kop.

As I was sitting there someone grabbed hold of my jersey. When the referee blew the whistle to try and play on I tried to get up but the fan still had hold of me and I over-balanced and fell right back into the crowd. It left the referee and 21 footballers looking for a goalkeeper! That summed up the general friendliness of it all. In the late 1960s there was a feeling that they wanted to make the opposition goalkeeper welcome. If you turned it on, they appreciated what you did.

JOHN OSBORNE
Ex-West Brom keeper

There was a guy in the Kop behind me and he said at full-time 'well played today, congratulations' and I thanked him.

Jamie Carragher came up and said something along the lines of 'you lucky so and so'. I just said, 'the harder I work the luckier I seem to get'. With all the tradition and stuff, Anfield is a great place to come and play. For Everton players it's even more special, especially to keep a clean sheet. I can remember being told to clap the Kop on my first visit to Anfield with Crystal Palace as they always give a good reception to goalkeepers. They still do today.

NIGEL MARTYN
Everton
keeper, 2004
after 0-0
Mersey derby
draw at Anfield

'The **fans** would stand together at **derby games** because they've got one thing **in common. They're** from the **same city**'

**Pigs might fly:
A great shot of Tommy
Lawrence in action at
Anfield in the 1960s.
Lawrence – famously
nicknamed 'The Flying
Pig' by the Kop –
dives to keep out a
Spurs effort in front
of the Kop in 1967**

**Top: Ray Clemence on
the receiving end on a
return trip to Anfield
with Spurs**

**Above: West Brom
keeper John Osborne
in action in front
of the Kop**

Shanks and Banks: The Kop gave a warm reception when Bill Shankly paraded England keeper Gordon Banks around Anfield before his retirement from the game. The Kop always loved class and Banks had a great rapport with Kopites

All eyes on the ball: This time Ray Clemence is powerless to prevent a Trevor Francis penalty from finding the net as the Kop looks on in 1978

When I first joined Liverpool I sat in the stand and marvelled at 20-odd thousand people singing and swaying together on the Kop.

Their humour was incredible and topical. The singing of 'You'll Never Walk Alone' was another experience.

I look back on the derby games I enjoyed but the win over St Etienne is the one which stands out.

It wasn't just the Kop which gave ultimate support that night. The whole stadium was gripped by a tremendous atmosphere.

My other memory is coming back to Anfield as a Spurs player for the first time. The reception I was given can only be described as a very emotional experience for myself.

But I have no individual memories because I closed my ears in order to concentrate on goalkeeping for 90 minutes. I heard deafening roars but that's all.

**RAY CLEMENCE
Liverpool legend**

The fans in the Kop when I came out . . . I will never, ever forget that. The applause I got was incredible although, to be fair to them, they had always given me a good reception when I was the away keeper.

It was very special and that summed the Kop up for me.

I could have gone down the road (to Portsmouth) for two years but that's why I'll never regret coming to Liverpool for a month.

Just to get that feeling.

**PAUL JONES
On-loan Liverpool keeper,
January 2004**

'We knew that we were living the dreams of the people watching'

Godsend: One Kopite sums up how we all felt about the playing genius of Kenny Dalglish

There was a unique bond between the people who stood on the terraces of the Kop and the players that they came to watch. It was a relationship that I believe was built on mutual respect.

The fans respected the players because they were successful. We won things almost every season and as a fan all you want for your team is for them to make you proud and to win silverware. The players gave their everything, every week and their efforts did not go unappreciated.

The Kop would accept defeat if it was defeat by a better team, because they were a sporting crowd but thankfully it was never something they had to get particularly used to.

There was no better lift when you were a goal down and chasing the game than the Kop in full voice.

They got us through some tricky times and that unswerving support was part of what endeared the support to the players.

But we, as players, also knew that we were living the dreams of the people watching from the stands.

They would have traded everything to be where we were so we wanted success for them as well as ourselves.

You would go that extra mile for them because they would go that extra mile for you in return. Playing in front of the Kop was an experience few people will ever forget.

**Sign of the times: An empty Kop provides the backdrop to
Kenny Dalglish's move from Celtic to Liverpool in 1977. It
wouldn't be long before the same terrace was packed to the
rafters proclaiming the new King of the Kop**

Kenny's done it: A famous Dalglish goal in front of the Kop, the second in a 3-1 comeback against Tottenham in May, 1982

Watching over us: An aerial view of Anfield as the Hillsborough carpet of flowers takes shape in 1989

Anfield at dawn: A groundsman surveys a silent Kop early one sunny morning in February, 1978

Glory daze: The silhouettes of ecstatic fans can be seen against the Kop windows after this Ian Rush goal at Anfield in September, 1985

Super Cally sends the Kop ballistic: Scoring against Inter Milan in 1965

'The magical night Liverpool arrived on the world stage'

ALAN EDGE

Author of 'Faith
Of Our Fathers'

On Tuesday, 4th May, 1965 Liverpool entertained World Club Champions Inter Milan in the semi-final first leg of the European Cup.

It was uncharted territory for the club and everyone connected with it.

The afternoon of the game half a dozen of us had skipped off school early to ensure that we would get in.

On the preceding Saturday, amidst pandemonium, the team had lifted the FA Cup for the first time in the club's history, so everyone knew the Milan game would be a lock-out.

Arriving at the ground at 4.30pm for the 7.30pm kick-off, by that time the queues were already enormous.

As we hurried frantically past the hordes queuing for the Kop along the Lake Street entry we caught wind that our intended destination, the boys' pen, was already closed.

At that point, we decided to try instead for the Kop end of the Paddock enclosure since we didn't fancy the length of the Kop queues.

Mercifully it proved to be a wise decision.

By 5.20pm we had squeezed inside. All the standing sections of the ground were already crammed tight so we must have been amongst the last in.

Such was our relief and exhilaration it felt as if we'd been the last through the pearly gates.

Certainly with St John on our side we can't have been that far from heaven.

Inside Anfield that night the terraces throbbed with an excitement I have never experienced before or since.

The buzz and tension tore at the nerve ends and sent untold adrenalin systems pumping wildly out of control.

Fifty five thousand were crammed inside. Possibly half that number was locked outside.

Controversy: In the away leg in Italy

The whole place bulged at the seams, threatening at any moment to burst apart like the crotch of Linford Christie's leotard.

It was an atmosphere that defied belief.

Over to our right was a 28,000 strong tidal wave of foaming humanity.

Scarcely two years earlier it had re-defined the parameters of football support.

Now, as it tumbled and cascaded back and forth for the entire night like the endless swelling ocean at Cape Horn, the Spion Kop was re-defining those parameters once again.

From the moment we squeezed in you simply could not take your eyes off the ceaseless swaying and movement.

Looking for all the world like some vast bank of windswept corn it drew your gaze and mesmerised you, making it virtually impossible to look away for more than a fleeting second in case you missed something.

The Kop was centre stage and determined to lap it up.

Prompted partly by the sheer inspiration of winning the FA Cup for the first time, partly by the ensuing celebrations and partly by a genuine apprehension and fear of the unknown - namely a European Cup semi-final and whether they would make it to the pub in time after the game - the Kopites rose to the occasion with a unique concoction of noise, fervour and humour, which not even they have since been able to match.

Joined by the rest of the stadium to wield a four-sided attack, they created an incessant four-hour barrage of chants, songs and sheer glorious bedlam.

Such was the din that a friend of mine later swore he was able to hear it in the city centre three miles away.

Giving their finest ever performance, they inspired their heroes to reciprocate and give theirs.

The chemistry of fans and team together proved potent and irresistible. ▶

▶ Raising the stakes with blatant propaganda, refrains of 'Ee-aye-addio Mussolini's dead' and 'We won the war' were pounded out time after time just in case any Italian visitors had conveniently forgotten events from twenty odd years earlier.

To add insult to insult the words of 'Santa Lucia' were also hastily re-written.

The unceasing strains of "Go-oh back to Italee" would reverberate round Latin heads for days afterwards. Who knows, perhaps forever?

Even before a ball had been spotted, the Italian World Champions had been frightened out of their skins.

The sheer ferocity of the reception they were accorded simply took the breath away.

Weaned as they were on hostile Latin crowds, it seemed even they had patently never encountered anything approaching the intensity present in the Anfield air that night.

As they ran out of the tunnel and headed towards the Kop end the waves of sound reached a crescendo, completely engulfing them.

The entire team seemed to stop in its tracks, rooted to the spot like petrified rabbits caught in the glare of a car's headlights.

Then, before this initial tumult had a chance to subside, injury victims Gordon Milne and Gerry Byrne ran round the running track with the FA Cup in a psychological ploy by Shankly to crank up the crowd's hysteria still further.

Once again, the Milan players scarcely knew what had hit them.

Understandably, they immediately turned tail and fled to the relative safety and calm of the Anfield Road end, their faces as shock-white as the hair on Don King's head.

In the stark contrast to Italian terror, the team in blood-red shirts were inspired to a pitch of frenzy to match that of the crowd.

They swarmed like possessed demons all over the poor bemused Italians and proceeded to tear them apart.

Once out of the dressing rooms, it had been even worse.

The Reds, simply, were unrecognisable.

We were all confident by that time that Liverpool were a really good side, probably even verging on greatness.

That, however, was by English, not top European or worldwide standards. And the Inter Milan team of Helenio Herrera were World Champions.

That night, however, the display the Reds unfolded was to amaze us all, reaching levels of performance that nobody had previously thought possible.

Beforehand, none of us had known what to expect. This was partly because we suspected the team might be tired from their extra-time exertions at Wembley and partly since we had no yardstick of our ability against a side of such panache as Inter Milan.

The unquestionable Milanese pedigree was enough to make even the most blinded die-hard question our chances.

Despite our FA Cup euphoria, the 'doubting Thomas's' amongst us - including myself - secretly dreaded from what we'd heard that our best might not be enough and we might just be cut to ribbons by these legendary counter attacking Italians. It was a fear that loomed large amongst many.

How wrong we were to harbour such reservations.

From the first kick the Italians were shredded like strings of spaghetti.

Every red pass found its red target, every red tackle shook Italian bones, every red surge tore past white shirted counterparts.

What stood out above all was the movement.

To quote John Travolta - who incidentally wasn't at the game - it was electrifying.

At times, it seemed as if the Italians were standing still and, who knows, maybe they were.

Each red shirt seemed to appear in half a dozen places at once.

> 'Even **before** a ball had been spotted, the Italian **World Champions** had been **frightened** out of their **skins. The sheer ferocity** of their reception took **the breath away'**

To provide a modern analogy, it looked for all the world as if somebody had released on to the pitch an army of supercharged Steven Gerrards on speed.

Peter Thompson and Cally were uncatchable the whole game, haring up and down the wings like . . . well, like hares, making Jair, the legendary Brazilian flier, look as if he'd just come out of some leaden-footed dream.

Up front, the Saint and 'Sir' Roger Hunt (though he wasn't formally knighted by the Kop for another year) played like we'd never seen before, tormenting the meanest defence football had yet witnessed, whose coach had once jokingly threatened to resign if they ever conceded more than one goal in a season.

In the middle, Willie 'Stevo' and Geoff Strong each discovered a couple of extra yards of pace and poured forward all night.

At the back, 'Big Rowdy' and Tommy Smith gobbled up any Inter attacking notions with Smithy for most of the time playing like the scheming number ten on his shirt and full-back Chris Lawler

looking like the best centre forward we'd ever had.

Ronnie Moran, meanwhile, was pretty baldy even then.

As for Tommy Lawrence, I'm not actually sure if he even bothered turning up.

Oh, how we battered them and oh, how we sang.

Barely a few minutes of red domination had passed before 'Sir' Roger, doing a Tiller Girl pirouette, hooked a little dink from Cally into the Anfield Road end net. Then after a further onslaught came a calamity. Inter Milan achieved what, otherwise, that night they found impossible.

They had an attack during which 'Big Rowdy' slipped up and Mazzola pulled a goal back.

Then it was back to normal service and the battering continued unabated. And through it all, so did our singing, chanting and swaying - even in the narrow strung out Paddock where the inhabitants must have looked like an elongated version of Bud Flanagan's 'Crazy Gang' on the stage at the London Palladium swaying to 'Underneath the ▶

**'With St John on our side, we can't have been far from heaven':
Hunt and St John celebrate the latter's goal against Inter Milan**

▶ Arches'.

Only we did it for four hours non-stop.

Then Cally scored from a free-kick move, the execution of which not even Melvyn Bragg has ever managed to figure out, let alone us mere mortals.

And evidently not Cally himself for he never ever tried it again.

Then, the Scarlet Pimpernel with a number two on his back tiptoed his way past the entire Milan defence and smacked one into the top corner but the referee disallowed it on the grounds - if I'm not mistaken - that an express UEFA directive forbade any team from scoring three goals in any one match against Inter Milan!

Still the battering went on and so did the singing and chanting and swaying.

Then, Tommy Smith came pouring forward through the descending mist with half a dozen white shirts clinging forlornly to his huge iron frame to put Sir Roger through to drive a shot against the keeper and in nipped the Saint to poke the rebound into the Kop net.

The referee took one look at the Kop's manic celebrations and decided - wisely I would say - to ignore the UEFA directive.

And that was that. Together in the end, the players, manager and fans had destroyed the best football team in the world.

That night, in truth, we would have overcome anyone or anything standing in our path; Rommell's Panzer Tank Division; ten battalions of warring Spartans; a fleet of Klingon Warships; Nigel Kennedy and his violin; even Eric Cantona in a bad mood - none would have stood a chance. All would have been annihilated. The fact was together we had achieved the ultimate footballing communion.

Manager, players and fans entirely as one; the united spirit and power of eleven plus fifty five thousand. Backed by half a city, of course. The sum infinitely greater than the parts. The Italians, in reality, never stood a chance.

The final score, 3-1, was a travesty of justice; it should have been at least 10-1, so total was the Red domination.

Eventually, long after the match had finished - by then fully four days after our Wembley FA Cup exultations - reluctantly and unwillingly, we all made our way home.

Desperate to prolong our high, we were still singing, still revelling, still savouring every last moment of our adventure. Sadly, inexorably, it was over; never to be repeated.

Since that time, in the wake of every ensuing Liverpool triumph, I have reflected, invariably, on that night in May 1965.

Whilst comparisons of this sort are inevitably invidious, so exceptional was that night I think special distinction is justified. Truth is everything else - no matter how great or important in its own right - really does tend to pale. That particular period in Liverpool Football Club's history truly was unique and it was the night of May 4th that heralded the club's arrival on the world stage.

All the ingredients crucial for so rich and rare an experience had been present: the unquenchable thirst for glory of all concerned with the club; a sense of inquisitiveness and trepidation concerning the then unknown Europe; the excitement and novelty of Sixties Liverpool and the first ever singing Kop; a truly formidable football team and a uniquely formidable manager and - most significantly of all - an overriding sense of anticipation that something truly momentous was happening to the club and us all that had never happened before.

For Liverpool fans, that night and the four days preceding it induced what must rank as one of the most sublimely fulfilled and sustained expressions of fandom imaginable. How fortunate and privileged we all had been. The intensity of joy and sense of communion went beyond the bounds of any reasonable expectations and dreams.

No Liverpudlian could ever have been even remotely hopeful of such a transcendent experience. No fan could.

And yet, it had happened.

Liverpudlians had been truly blessed and we would all take with us to our graves the indelible and priceless memories.

Players, manager and fans alike.

Meanwhile those who weren't there, I'm afraid, will just have to take my word for it or else dismiss what I have said as the ramblings of a man stranded in a time warp with a propensity for making absurd exaggerations and no doubt getting on non-Liverpudlian nerves.

And why not?

**Knighted by the Kop: Roger Hunt celebrates another goal in front of the
fans who called him 'Sir' – this time against Chelsea in 1966**

Liverpool were back into the First Division. We got into Europe for the first time; it was something that was new.

Everything was on the up and the spectators were absolutely unbelievable. Every game was a sell-out.

For me, the Inter Milan match was the greatest atmosphere I ever played in at Anfield.

Gerry Byrne and Gordon Milne paraded the FA Cup because that was the first time that we had won it.

To come back a few days later and play against Inter Milan and beat Inter Milan was something else.

The atmosphere before the game when we came out on the pitch was incredible.

'SIR' ROGER HUNT

When the team ran out with the FA Cup just before the game you just knew it was going to be an immortal night. That's the only way to describe it.

We were watching history in the making.

**DAVID MOORES
Liverpool Chairman**

It was fantastic to play in front of it. There was 28,000 on the Kop and the atmosphere was incredible.

It was the humour as well, the things that they sang.

It was a marvellous place to play.

**IAN CALLAGHAN
Scorer v Inter Milan**

The ties that bind: A Juventus banner on the Kop. The two clubs developed a special bond after the tragedy of the 1985 Heysel disaster

Champs again: The 1986 title winning side celebrates with the Kop

'I ended up in Alder Hey with three broken ribs – but it was worth it!'

The first time I ever stood at Anfield was in the Anfield Road end - in the visitors' section.

It was Easter Monday 1986 and Liverpool were at home to Manchester City and my dad had promised to take me on the Kop for the first time after years of watching the Reds from the Main Stand.

We queued up for almost an hour but 10 minutes before kick-off the Kop gates were closed and we were turned away. Being a resourceful chap, and with a heart-broken 10-year-old in his company, my dad decided to go around to the City end to try and get in there.

Despite having accents more Fairfield than Fallowfield we got in and watched Liverpool go top of the league thanks to two Steve McMahon goals.

I say watched, but the truth is the only thing I watched was the Kop. It was one of those special days when the League Championship loomed on to the horizon and the Kop was at its best.

Watching Liverpool wasn't good enough for me - I wanted to stand on the Kop. Our next home game was about a week later against Coventry and I was determined not to miss out again.

We queued up even earlier this time and got on to the terrace just as the Sayers cafe at the back of the Kop opened up. There were only a few people there - it was 1.30pm after all - but just being there was enough. As it started filling up and the Kopites began belting out their songs, I knew it was the only place for me. ▶

Home alone: Steve McMahon during a reserves run-out with a perfect view of the 1980s' Kop in the background

▶ Liverpool won 5-0 that day and I've been on the Kop ever since.

Some of the most memorable moments in my life took place on that vast, somewhat ugly construction of concrete and wood. My most vivid recollection is of breaking my ribs when I got squashed against a crush barrier during a derby game in 1987-88.

That was the season of Barnes, Beardsley and Aldridge - the greatest team I've ever seen. You had to queue up four hours before kick-off just to have a chance of getting in that year. But it only cost £1.80 on the kids' gate to enjoy some of the most free-flowing football played in the history of the British game. You can't even get a pie at the match for that price anymore!

Having gone in through the kids' gate I got separated from my dad but I knew where we stood at the back of the Kop and thought I would make my way up there. But I chose the wrong route. I took the shortest path - through the middle of the Kop.

At first I was happy to be stuck in the throng because I was at the heart of all the action.

The noise was incredible and with the constant swaying my feet were literally not touching the ground.

The game kicked off and Liverpool went straight on the attack and the Kop surged forward. Being 11 and about six and a half stone I couldn't really hold off 8,000 people at my back and I got trapped against a barrier. The pain was unbearable but then Peter Beardsley cracked a half volley in off the underside of the crossbar and everything went mad.

As everyone celebrated I was able to free myself and even forgot the pain for a minute as I joined in with the pandemonium.

But as the game wore on the pain grew worse and worse and I can't remember seeing the rest of the match.

I ended up in Alder Hey with three broken ribs but it had all been worth it.

Liverpool had beaten Everton but, even more importantly, I had graduated to the middle of the Kop.

In Italy it would be the place for the Ultras, the most fanatical supporters of the clubs in Serie A.

And at Anfield it was no different.

The stands always seemed a bit stuffy, there was no singing and supporters would do little more than clap when Liverpool scored - a sort of retirement home for ex-Kopites.

The middle of the Kop had a mind of its own. It was where songs started and where fans in the rest of the ground looked to for inspiration.

Although its best days had gone by the late '80s (according to everyone who had been there in the '60s anyway) there was still a buzz about the place.

My favourite memories are of watching one of Liverpool's finest ever performances, as we brushed Nottingham Forest aside in a stunning 5-0 victory.

Also, being in a crowd of 22,000 - most of whom were on the Kop - as we overturned a first-leg two goal deficit to beat Auxerre 3-0 in the UEFA Cup.

The spartan crowd that night was obviously made up of die-hards because despite being only half-full the atmosphere was incredible.

I think the other 20,000 who didn't turn up must be the ones who never sing because the noise level didn't suffer without them.

The last day of the Kop as we knew it was a strange occasion.

Getting beaten by Norwich didn't help but it was a happy/sad affair with the sight of so many banners heralding past glories and some of the older songs serenading the end of a truly great institution.

The Kop mark-two is not the same.

It still has the ability to truly inspire the team like no other stand in the country as countless European visitors can testify. I still sit in the middle of the Kop but more often than not you hear people muttering instead of singing and at times it is as quiet as Sunday morning Mass.

It reminds me of an aging boxer who was once King of the world but hasn't got the legs to make things happen anymore. But it has never lost its punch and every now and again can deliver a real knockout blow.

Just ask Roma.

'The **pain was unbearable** but then Peter Beardsley cracked a **half volley** in off the underside of the bar and everything **went mad'**

'Kopites are football people'

The night Arsenal won the league at Anfield was the most memorable game I've ever played in. The way it turned out, it was one of those games to never be repeated.

Before that game Anfield had always been a lucky ground for me when I was at Leicester. We were something of a bogey team for Liverpool.

I scored twice at Anfield one season although I think we lost that day. Ian Rush might have scored three and Liverpool ended up winning 4-3.

It was always a ground I loved playing on because it was such a football arena.

I remember the first couple of times I played at Anfield. I'd heard so much about the famous Kop and I remember just standing in front of it when I was attacking or defending a corner and feeling the hot air coming off it.

The Kop was standing and packed back then and standing so close to it and feeling that hot air was fantastic.

The Kop were always great to us, especially on that night in 1989.

The game wasn't long after Hillsborough and before it we presented the crowd with flowers to show our respects. I think it was George Graham's idea to do that and obviously it did us no harm.

We won the game 2-0 to win the title but, even though they were disappointed, the applause we got from not only the Kop but the whole stadium meant an awful lot to be honest.

It made it more special than it already was because I think everyone recognises that Liverpool fans are football people and people who know their football. Even if an opposing player produces a piece of skill you'd always hear a ripple of applause. Players notice that.

I think they recognised that we'd given it our best shot to win the game and the reception we got was fantastic.

I can remember the Kop trying to get the ref to blow his whistle early. They started whistling for the final whistle a good five or ten minutes before the end. There was no clock at Anfield in those days so we didn't know how long there was to go.

It went on and on but then Michael Thomas got the goal right at the end.

Tribute: Kevin Richardson and Perry Groves present the crowd with flowers. Above: A fan helps a disconsolate John Barnes back on his feet

I think we went up there more in hope than expectation of winning that night. None of the papers that morning had given us a chance of going up there and winning 2-0 so in many respects the pressure was off. My goal gave us a platform and we got the winner but I don't suppose anyone expected it to happen.

I scored the winner in the 1994 European Cup Winners Cup Final against Parma and that was a very special night for me. But from the team's point of view, that night in 1989 was the greatest.

Even the lads who went on to play under Arsene Wenger and did the double still go back to the night in 1989 and think it's never going to get any better than that. It was just really special.

Walk On: The Kop in
full song in May, 1989

'Many golden memories

Fans who visit Anfield and take the official tour are taken into the present all-seater Kop. People actually find it quite an emotional and thrilling experience, even though they are sitting in an empty stadium.

If I try to be dispassionate, it is just a stand, but visitors get very excited about sitting in one of those 12,000 seats and looking out across Anfield.

I've even known one or two to break into song!

If you then go into the museum itself, you can actually take your place on a piece of the old standing Kop and watch a film that depicts what is was like to be a standing supporter on this legendary football terrace.

The film takes you from the early days and comes right up to date, highlighting what was a really emotional occasion when Gerard Houllier made his first appearance after the illness that nearly took his life.

That day, all the Kop held up cards that formed a giant mosaic in tribute of our manager.

As part of the museum experience, we try to get across the noise, the passion, the singing, the banter and the jokes that made the Kop stand out in the world of football.

Some of the great personalities are on film, talking about their experiences and their memories.

We try to make a point that the old standing Kop, for all the right reasons in the aftermath of the agony that was Hillsborough, had to change and has changed.

In the film, the screen goes dark and then the Kop lights up, re-born in a different way as the giant structure we know today.

Football had to move forward for all the right safety reasons and in memory of the 96 passionate Liverpudlians who died in Sheffield. There is no going back, but then the modern Kop remains a very special place.

Our video shows Steven Gerrard scoring and the modern all-seater Kop cheering to the rafters. It makes you realise that the Kop is alive and well and that is very important. It's particularly important for our young visitors who never stood on the old Kop and can only imagine what it was like.

They still feel that the Kop they sit in is amazing, but in a different way.

The Kop can still explode in a sea of colour and be an inspirational sight.

Equally, it's wonderful that thousands of people have vivid memories of the way it was.

We actually have a large chunk of concrete that formed one of the steps on the old Kop.

People can actually stand on it and begin to imagine what it must have been like.

We also have some decorative bricks from the outside facing.

I think it was important that we kept something of what was a football institution.

Of course, when the Kop was

The Kop lives on: An original Kop turnstile in the Liverpool Museum – along with ex-Reds star and current public relations manager Brian Hall; Brookside writer Phil Redmond and stars from the former soap; Mike McCartney, Liverpool legend Alan Kennedy and Gerry Marsden

of **glory days** gone by'

The way it was: A corner view of the early Spion Kop as seen from Walton Breck Road and Lake Street

broken into thousands of pieces, someone had a great idea to use the bits of rock to raise money for charity, specifically the Hillsborough Support Group, and many of those pieces were mounted with clocks and all manner of (rather kitsch) things.

We actually have quite a large fragment surrounded by two Liver Birds. It was sold as a souvenir and donated back to the museum.

Within our museum, we also have a special banner given to us by a supporter. It states: "KOP, REST IN PEACE, 1994" .

It was held high on the Kop in the weeks leading to the famous Last Stand.

The owner feels it is not appropriate to take it on the Kop now and so it will reside in the museum forever.

In 1972, a record was made featuring the 'Kop Choir'. The singing is inspirational and has never been bettered by any other club. It sold so many that

the club was presented with a Gold Disc and we still have it. These were the days when the Beatles and Merseybeat music had taken the world by storm.

Liverpool was the centre of the universe at that time and the Kop was the centre of that footballing universe. Of course, it was just a stand made of concrete and metal, but it was the people within it that made it come alive.

We have the matchday programme from the Kop's Last Stand against Norwich.

It is signed by all the players, fittingly in red.

What makes it extra special is that the immortal Billy Liddell was here that day and he added his signature.

In the early Seventies, it became popular amongst a group of ardent supporters from Skelmersdale to dress up in white boiler suits adorned with all manner of things, each fan also wearing a giant comedy top hat made out of cardboard. ▶

123

Glimpses of the past: Two views of the early Kop. One from a drawing showing the Main Stand and corner of the Kop and (top) a museum model of Anfield

▶ We have two of these boiler suits, worn on the Kop and at the old Wembley Stadium.

They are a tribute to the humour and personality of the Kop.

In the Kop film, one of the most spine tingling things is footage of the great Liddell scoring a goal in front of the Kop in the Fifties.

The crowd can be heard roaring: "There's only one Billy Liddell".

Nothing has changed. Every decade had its heroes.

The Kop was not suddenly invented in the Sixties although this is the era most people relate to when they think about the standing Kop.

We actually have a wooden rattle that we think was carried on the Kop before the first World War, pre-1914.

Written on it are the words: "You will hear us every Saturday," and so Kopites have clearly been fiercely proud of their passion for the best part of a century.

Of course, the Kop came alive after the Second World War when there was a massive resurgence in attendances at football matches. The game was very affordable then and it helped at Anfield when the side of 1946/47 won the first post-war Championship.

The all-time record attendance at Anfield was 61,905, achieved when Liverpool met Wolverhampton in the fourth round of the FA Cup on February 2nd, 1952.

Can you imagine how many actually stood on the Kop that day? It must have been truly remarkable.

We all remember famous nights like St Etienne in 1977, but can you begin to imagine the noise on that day in 1952?

Liddellpool FC: Billy Liddell on a sunny day at Anfield in the 1950s with the famous Kop windows in the distant background. Below: Fancy dress from the same era helps fans to get in the mood

'One of the most **spine tingling** things is footage of the great **Billy Liddell scoring** a goal in front of the Kop in **the Fifties'**

Above us only sky! The original Kop without a roof (above) and a shot from 1928, with a roof being built

Two images from the 1960s (top) as the roof is rebuilt and (above) the roof of the new all-seater Kop going on in 1994

'The Kop went absolutely crazy, like steam was coming out of their ears'

The first time I officiated at Anfield I was running the line. It was Liverpool versus Burnley, sometime in the mid '70s. I remember my first visit well.

Tom Reynolds was the referee and during the game Steve Heighway came down the left wing and played it off a player. The ball went out for a corner kick, which I quite happily gave.

Tom Reynolds though, a bearded Welshman, gave a goal kick. The Kop went absolutely crazy. It was like steam was coming out of their ears.

I remember distinctly Reynolds, having given very firmly a goal-kick, hear the crowd's reaction. He shrugged his shoulders, looked in my direction and gave a corner kick. He got a ripple of applause after that. I realised that night the weight of the Kop.

On another occasion I arrived at Anfield and a steward ushered me up into a lounge area and asked me if I wanted my photograph taken?

I looked around and there, on the window-sill, was the European Cup, the League Championship and the Charity Shield. A week later I got the photograph back and I've kept that as a treasured momento.

Things like that have made Anfield a very special place for me.

The likes of Peter Robinson, who was a perfect gentleman, and Sir John Smith would always come into my dressing room and wish me every success.

There is a tradition of treating match officials in a very professional manner. Even now I'll go back and have a chat with Ronnie Moran.

But I've always enjoyed going to Liverpool, mainly because of the friendliness of the spectators.

I have a strong passion for the game and they share that.

Just walking down the steps and seeing 'This is Anfield' and running on to the pitch and seeing the wall of spectators . . . just an absolute wall singing 'You'll Never Walk Alone' was something special.

Every time I hear it, even today, it brings a lump to my throat. As someone who comes from Sheffield, I'm sure you'll understand why.

I don't think the Kop ever influenced my decisions but they gave me a lift. Officiating at Anfield gave me an adrenalin rush because you knew you were at somewhere special.

I'm not a religious guy but there was always some kind of reverence - it's difficult to describe really - about Anfield.

I was very lucky that I never got any real animosity thrown at me there. I always looked forward to refereeing at Anfield and even now, in my capacity as acting select group manager for Premiership referees, I still very much enjoy going there because it's retained everything about a true football stadium. The passion and the friendliness is still there.

Before a game I used to have to walk round and check the nets. When I was down at the Kop end checking the nets I always knew that I was in a sense walking on true, hallowed turf.

On one occasion in midweek I arrived very early for a game and they were actually scattering the ashes of a fan around the goal area and at the back.

That was quite a touching ceremony and I remember seeing the family quietly having a discussion with Bill Shankly.

I refereed Workington's last match in the

Changing seasons: A referee's inspection at a snowy Anfield in 1985 and (left) a view of the seated Kop as the pitch is relaid during the 1990s

Football League and the groundsman there told me how Shankly used to drive the tractor and cut the grass!

Shortly afterwards I was at Anfield and told him the story but Shankly was more bemused that I'd refereed at Workington recently and was now at Anfield and about to referee a top first division game!

I was also very lucky to referee the likes of Kenny Dalglish. Whenever I'm asked who was the best player in the world that I refereed, I always say Dalglish.

I've refereed Maradona, Platini, Rummenigge and Best but for me Dalglish had everything. He was a winner and what a fantastic player.

I refereed John Charles' testimonial - Leeds v Juventus - and Kenny actually played. Three minutes before the final whistle he put a superb ball through to this young lad who gave up on it.

Dalglish was into him like a rocket and gave him an absolute blasting. That was the Liverpool way.

My very last game as a referee was Man United v Liverpool at Old Trafford in 1994.

I gave Liverpool a penalty but the linesman said I'd got it wrong and it should have been a free-kick the other way. So I turned the penalty down and came off. Roy Evans came into my dressing room and said 'Isn't it about time you retired?', to which I quietly replied 'Actually Roy this is my last game'.

My colleagues were absolutely gobsmacked. I'd been coming up a bit short and had decided prior to kick-off that it would be my last game. I was just pleased to go out refereeing two great teams.

I go back to Anfield now and still see the same faces I saw in the '70s. That says a lot for the club.

I've got a lot of memories of the Kop and the really memorable thing about officiating there was when I'd go mid-season, sort of late November.

It was usually dark, overcast and there was almost a mist rising up in front of the floodlights.

The atmosphere would seem to go up a bit on those nights and a lot of people who see Anfield now, since the change to the Kop, find it quite difficult to picture what the Kop was like.

It was just a sea of faces, a sea of passion and I'd just walk around the pitch and think 'Crikey, what a stadium'.

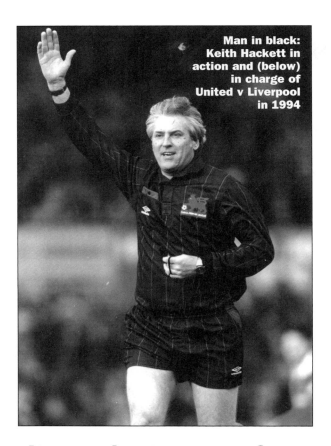

Man in black: Keith Hackett in action and (below) in charge of United v Liverpool in 1994

'It was just a **sea of faces**, a sea of **passion** and I'd just walk around the pitch and think 'Crikey, what a stadium''

Legend of 'Scouse Columbo'

As a Kop season ticket holder throughout the '90s I, like many Kopites, have many great memories of the famous old stand.

I could go on about the Auxerre's, Genoa's and Roma's, plus the banter we've all experienced and taken part in at some point but this particular recollection actually occurred on our way to the ground.

The hilarity of what was witnessed was typical of many of the sights and, more importantly here, sounds encountered along the way and sent us into Anfield in tears of laughter as we assumed 'our' usual spot on what was still the old terrace at the time.

Remember Columbo? The famous old hardboiled detective played by Peter Falk, but more famously in my eyes his Scouse double who used to (and maybe still does) sell burgers and hotdogs from his stall outside Anfield.

'Scouse Columbo' was a local legend with me and my mates for over a decade, and as we trudged through Stanley Park onto Anfield Road, the anticipation always grew as to whether he would be there in his 'pitch' between Skerries Road and the Shankly Gates.

Of course, he always was with his knee length Columbo coat on (only in hotdog vendors white instead of camel brown, plus the obligatory mustard stains, of course) and the famous cigar had been replaced by a cigarette - great with ketchup I believe!

This day, it must have been about 1991-92 - I can't remember the match but that's incidental. Out of The Park we emerged as one of the lads spots our hero: "There he is, there's Columbo, never let's us down..."

As we got closer to him the usual buzz of his presence flowed through us, but this time it was to be special as 'Scouse Columbo' implanted himself firmly in our memories forever - and how!

None deterred by the waft of boiled onions, we shuffled alongside him to get as close as possible but as we drew near, our man looked to be composing himself for something big.

The Kop: Home to an interesting mix of sights, sounds . . . and smells!

Bending his knees and crouching forward, 'Scouse Columbo' proceeded to let rip one of the loudest farts you could wish to hear.

Forget those nasty silent things you would have to endure on the Kop with no warning whatsoever after some docker had downed 20 pints of bitter the night before, this was the real deal.

With a pained grimace spread across his face, 'Scouse Columbo' then turned to his arse and with a waft of his hand uttered quite simply "Get out and walk yer b****** . . ."

This was absolute poetry in motion, and as we burst into fits of laughter, our hero rubberstamped his legend status with a quick wink (with his good eye) and a smirk in our direction before getting back to work: "Get yer burgers and hotdogs 'ere..."

Not today thanks Columbo, but you'll always be a Kop legend in our eyes mate.

'With a **final flourish,** the

The Kop is unique amongst football phenomena; probably the most famous football terrace in the world. But that fame has only been achieved since the 1960s.

For the first half of the century, it regularly contained tens of thousands of Liverpudlians - mostly dock workers and labourers - who were certainly some of the most vociferous fans in the land, but who were not perhaps so different from the other huge banks of working men who stood behind the goals of so many British clubs.

It was the Sixties and after that transformed the Kop into an institution of world football. Those of us lucky enough to be born in time to witness those early days of Shankly's reign, when the club and the city's popular culture seemed to rise together in perfect union, will never forget it. There is nothing like the

first time, taking Europe by surprise, winning the FA Cup. We felt, as Shankly put it, 'on a rocket ship bound for the moon'. As local groups turned out hit records with the same regularity that the football team led its rivals, something happened on the Kop which changed the culture of football's terraces, first in Britain and eventually throughout the world.

In the old days, football crowds had sometimes sung before matches, to the accompaniment of a local brass band perhaps, but during the game it was the roar of the crowd which everyone remembered.

In the Sixties, as if in celebration of the city's pre-eminent position in the music world, the Kop began first to adopt, then to adapt the hit song of the period to the events and characters on the pitch.

Thanks to the simultaneous arrival of TV coverage of football matches, everyone heard it. Soon everyone was at it. Songs would get minted on the Kop one week and be heard at another ground the next.

Kop told itself to sit down'

From us to you: The players unfurl a banner to the Kop on the 'Last Stand' day in 1994

One song in particular became a communal anthem. After the Kop adopted it wholesale, all Britain's football fans knew they would never walk alone.

Some of the best memories of my life have been on the Kop. In my 'Desert Island' list of memories, apart from the St Etienne game in 1977 (which everyone who attended carries engraved on their hearts), the Grimsby Town match in early 1980 stands out as an example of the Kop at its wittiest.

Not content with clever choruses of 'you only sing when you're fishing', and with the match well won before half-time, bored Kopites decided to liven up the game by giving the entire Liverpool team 'fishy' names, starting with 'Oh Jimmy, Jimmy, Jimmy, Jimmy, Jimmy, Jimmy, Jimmy Plaice'. They worked their way through 'Kenny Dogfish', 'Phil Seal', 'Stingray Kennedy' etc and we nearly died laughing.

I'll never forget Tommy Smith's testimonial either. It was in 1977, just a few days after the great

pilgrimage to Rome, where Smithy had scored the second goal with a wonderful header. He couldn't have timed his well-deserved pay night better.

The place was heaving with some still under the influence of Roman vino. That night witnessed one of the strangest pieces of mass theatre the Kop has ever performed. It began with a light-hearted attempt to make the (then standing) fans in the Anfield Road end sit down. The Kop sang 'Annie Road, Annie Road, all sit down' . . . and to everyone's amazement they did.

Much encouraged, the Kop turned to the Kemlyn Road and instructed everyone there to stand up. They obeyed immediately. Now thoroughly warmed to the task, the Kopites sought the next prime target - the directors' box. We all wondered: would the camel coats stand up too? Sure enough, they did.

With a final flourish, and with a gesture that now seems prophetic, the Kop told itself to sit down.

And we did.

133

'The banter, the noise, the songs, the chants, the humour – it was fabulous'

I remember the first time I came across the Kop. It was in 1962, the year they went up to the First Division, and they had an epic FA Cup tie with Preston North End.

Preston were a good side at the time and had Peter Thompson playing for them. They drew at Anfield, drew at Preston and went to Manchester for a third game which Preston won by a Thompson goal.

But we were invaded at Preston by Liverpool fans on the night of the second game. It's one of the most memorable football nights I ever had. It was incredible.

The banter, the noise, the songs, the chants, the humour - it was just absolutely fabulous.

By 1965 I'd signed on as an amateur and after training Reuben Bennett came to us and said 'I've got some passes if you want to watch the game tonight'. It was a European game, I can't remember who against, and I got there for half-time.

We went on the paddock and I spent most of the 45 minutes watching the Kop. I'd never seen anything like it in my life. It was absolutely phenomenal. The songs, the noise and the steam coming off it - it was just out of this world.

I only ever went on the Kop once. I was an amateur player while I was at university and we were playing Manchester United who had Bobby Charlton, George Best, Denis Law and all the rest in their team.

One of my pals at university was 6ft 6. He was an enormous guy and a Manchester United fan. He asked if there was any chance of getting some tickets but I told him I couldn't get tickets for the Kop. I didn't have a game that afternoon so we went and queued.

So we went on the Kop. We didn't get anywhere near the middle but even so I hardly saw a damn thing. I'm 5ft 5 and a bit and I couldn't see a bloody thing. I spent the 90 minutes listening to my 6ft 6 mate giving me a commentary!

It was a fantastic experience though and I remember more about that experience of being on the Kop than I do of the match itself.

The Kop family: Liverpool fans have always shared in the players' achievements on and off the pitch – in this case Ian Callaghan earns the plaudits for his MBE

I can't remember my first game at Anfield but one which stands out was when we played Everton in November 1970. It was my first derby match and there was about five or six of us who hadn't played in derbies before.

Everton had a terrific side and we were the up and coming new side so I suppose they were favourites really. The atmosphere in the stadium when I ran out was electric. There were red and blue

High life of Brian: Hall – or 'Little Bamber' as he was known – celebrates with the Kop

scarves everywhere, all over the stadium, and the atmosphere was wonderful.

Within about 10 minutes of the second half we were two down. We were getting beaten 2-0 at Anfield to Everton but the Kop stayed with us. They kept singing and urging us on.

When our first one went in there was a hell of a din. When our second one went in there was an unbelievable din. And when our third one went in, I'll tell you what, you couldn't hear yourself think.

We'd run back to the centre-circle and I was in the middle of the pitch and tried to say something to Chris Lawler, who'd scored the winner, but I couldn't hear myself. It was phenomenal. There were fans on the Kop roof and all sorts. I think the official capacity was about 55,000 but there was 60 odd thousand in there that day. ▶

'It was a very **daunting** experience for teams when they **came to us.** They knew they were going to **meet** this **barrage** of sound'

Man of the people: Shanks with his beloved fans

The Kop were part and parcel of the 'This is fortress Anfield' thing. It wasn't just the 10 red and one green shirts that ran out to play, it was the Kop as well. We were all in it together. It was a very daunting experience for teams and individual players when they came to us. They knew they were going to meet this barrage of sound.

The European nights were special. I always felt that Anfield in particular had a fantastic sense of theatre on floodlit games. The arena was lit, the crowd were literally three yards from your shoulder on the touchline and there was all the noise and colour. There was a huge piece of theatre taking place and that was accentuated by the floodlighting.

In those days we didn't know what to expect from the opposition and neither did the crowd. There was like an air of expectancy but also a sense of going into the unknown. When we'd overcome that unknown, it made it extra special. There was an edge to it and those nights were great.

I kind of rationalise it though. The Kop wasn't worth a goal start. The lads on the park had to put the ball in the back of the net but the Kop was very much an integral part of the event.

My understanding is that when Bill Shankly first came to Liverpool he felt something for the place. I think he actually saw himself there. He was so passionate about his football and he saw passionate people standing on the terraces who expressed their passion very openly. I think that's a trait of Liverpool people. They are very open, they are very honest, they do tell you what they think and often wear their hearts on their sleeves.

Bill could see that within the support. He saw their passion and saw that he was one of them. He came from a small mining village and a lot of people who came to the stadium had a difficult or poor upbringing. There was a lot of common ground that he empathised with. He'd do little things like stand at the players entrance on a match day and give out a few complimentary tickets here, there and everywhere to the kids. Those little stories used to get about so I think people looked back to Shanks and saw themselves. He's one of us.

'Moments frozen in time'

Like its musical equivalent of seeing the Clash play at Eric's it was the game that even those who weren't there would swear was their greatest ever 'live' experience.

But 'early darts' arrival at three in the afternoon was not enough to get in and with an hour to go the gates were locked and I was still outside.

The game? It was 1977, the night of Supersub, and watching Fairclough's winning goal against St Etienne on the TV later was not enough to blunt one of the most bitter sweet emotions of my life and the ache felt on not being there to make the difference.

That's what being a fan on the terraced Kop used to mean - a suspension of disbelief in Shankly's old adage that we could actually suck the ball into the opponents' net by the sheer volume of our support.

I knew it to be true - I'd actually been lucky enough to be there to see it happen the season before.

Crushed in the favourite spec just below the narrow plateau halfway up and 20 degrees off the left-hand goal post, we'd watched Bruges emphatically put us in our place in the first leg of the UEFA Cup Final.

Lambert and Cools had crashed two great goals past Clemence and come half-time we were down, outplayed and almost out.

Except for the K factor . . .

The chanting - a kind of low rumble - had already begun as the last man left the pitch. Ten minutes later as Jensen, the Bruges keeper, nervously limbered up between the Kop sticks the noise had become not so much a wall of sound as a psychopathic yowl, a collective clenched fist of defiance.

There was an incredible feeling that despite the deficit nothing - but nothing - was going to stop us turning this around. That recollection even now sends a delicious shiver of power shooting down the back of the spine.

And so it came to pass. Ray Kennedy clubbed in a 20-yard net buster on the hour.

Two minutes later he nearly did it again when the shot hit the post and Jimmy Case, who'd been brought on for Toshack at the break, slotted home the rebound.

Two-all and the ears were threatening to explode, the voice had cracked and the breath gone thanks to hyperventilation and frequent collisions between the solar plexus and the crush barrier as we swayed back and forth like a mad tsunami.

Then Bastyns chopped down Heighway in the area and Keegan stepped up to take the penalty.

Bedlam, and many couldn't bear to watch as Mighty Mouse coolly placed the ball and smashed it home.

I went down in the crush of bodies.

Seconds later the wave receded and briefly I was left on my knees in a briefly empty space hugging my twin brother laughing and crying at the same time in the sheer bonkers ecstasy of it all.

These are moments that will forever be frozen in time. And when my dreams are being tossed and blown as they seem to be all too frequently these days, I think back to that night for a little solace - and quietly celebrate at being a small part of what once were giants.

> 'The **ears were threatening to explode,** the voice **had cracked and the breath gone** thanks **to hyperventilation** and **frequent collisions** between **the solar plexus and the crush barrier** as **we swayed back** and **forth'**

One of us: Players sometimes end up in the Kop unintentionally. In this rare archive pic, it's Kevin Keegan who was warmly welcomed by the Anfield faithful when he arrived unannounced in the crowd against Slask Wroclaw in December, 1975

'Anfield **erupted. The** place **went berserk, it** was **pure bedlam'**

'The Match is worth logging into the memory bank because once the Kop has become all-seater, I doubt whether we will ever witness such passion and commitment from a crowd again'
Manchester Evening News
January, 1994

I could smell it in the air as I walked up Walton Breck Road. It was like a crackling of electricity was passing through the night air and charging Liverpool supporters on their way up to the ground.

I had a sense of excitement and anticipation but it was tempered with a sense of trepidation.

Evening games against Manchester United at Anfield are always more volatile. More highly charged.

But this was to be the last time they would come to Anfield and play in front of the old Spion Kop.

I just had a gut feeling that we were in for something special, a night to remember.

It was still an hour before kick off but I could hear the noise from the Kop filtering down Walton Breck Road.

That had never happened before. Not since I'd been going to Anfield.

My first game was in January 1987 but that is the one and only occasion I can remember hearing such a noise before I could even see The Albert.

I wasn't on the Kop that night. By then I'd got my season ticket in the Paddock - Kop end of course - and had become an avid admirer rather than a participant.

I've always loved the moment when I walk through the little tunnel-like area that leads you from inside the concourse to the Paddock seats.

It's the moment when, as you fight your way past the Bovril buyers, you catch a glimpse of the luscious green turf for the first time.

It's just a glimpse, mind, but a glimpse that leaves you wanting more. It's Anfield's equivalent of cleavage.

It doesn't give you that same breath-taking, awe-inspiring moment when you reach the top of the old Kop steps for the first time and see the Kop but, none the less, it was always enough to get me buzzing.

Not that I needed anything to get me buzzing that night.

As I walked out of that Paddock tunnel the noise slapped me in the face like a wet mackerel. It was astonishing.

The Kop looked full. Rammed. I just stood there, frozen to the spot, like I'd never been inside Anfield before.

There they were, enjoying an almighty old school sing-song despite the fact that we were playing our hated rivals who were strolling to their second title in a row and could, quite conceivably, give us a thrashing.

I looked towards the Mancs in the Annie Road end and most of their seats were full. That's the way it is when you're a Manc at Anfield or a Scouser at Old Trafford.

You don't hang around for long outside the ground and, true to form, the Mancs hadn't.

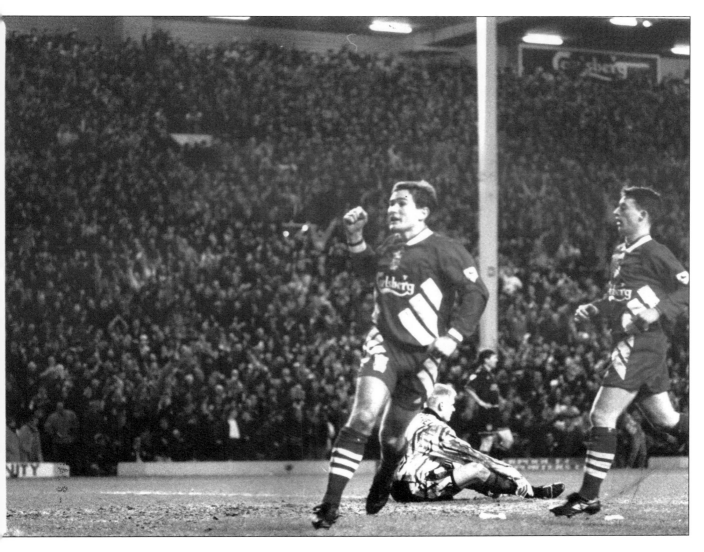

Instead they were stood or sat in silence as the sea of red and white opposite made more noise than they had ever heard at their place. And this was before a ball had even been kicked.

Moments before the teams came out, DJ George played 'You'll Never Walk Alone' over the PA system.

He could have switched it off after the first word because no-one could hear Gerry Marsden.

As I held my scarf aloft my eyes were firmly focused on the Kop.

All of a sudden, the sea of scarves and flags were joined by two blazing red flares, which sent plooms of red smoke pouring towards the sky.

It was a beautiful sight. An image I, and I dare say the Sky viewers tuning into the game at home, will never forget.

Had the Kop ever been more colourful?

United won the toss and, not surprisingly, turned us round.

The boos and howls of derision hadn't died down by the time Peter Schmeichel, with a nose as red as Liverpool's shirts, made his way down to the Kop end.

Twenty-three minutes later and the only colourful thing I was aware of was the language around me.

United were 3-0 up and had, temporarily, silenced the Kop.

Early goals from Steve Bruce and Ryan Giggs had been met by an increase in volume but Dennis Irwin's third - a free-kick that seemed to make an almighty 'clunk' on the way in - was met with silence.

It lasted 90 seconds.

With the United fans still celebrating, Nigel Clough smashed in an unbelievable 30-yard shot that had us all believing again.

The noise levels exploded into life and, if I'm ▶

▶ not mistaken, another flare or two lit up the Kop.

Clough got a second before half-time and by now the ground was rocking.

United had turned from arguably the best visiting side we'd seen for years into quivering wrecks. They were all over the place. The noise ebbed and flowed with the game in the second half. Maybe it is just a psychological thing, maybe it's true, but Anfield never seems quite as loud when Liverpool aren't attacking the Kop in the second half. Liverpool cranked up the pressure and with 11 minutes to go Neil Ruddock headed home Stig Inge Bjornebye's cross. It was like he'd dropped a tonne of dynamite into a volcano.

Anfield erupted. The place went beserk. I can't even remember the last 10 minutes – it was pure bedlam. Shortly after the final whistle sounded, 'You'll Never Walk Alone' rang around the ground as good as I've ever heard it. Everyone was engulfed in the moment. The Mancs, made to stay behind by the police so they could be safely escorted to their coaches, had to just sit there and watch.

That was quickly followed by an impromptu and hugely ironic rendition of 'Always Look on the Bright Side of Life' that was directed towards the away end.

Some people in the Paddock who I'd never seen move, let alone sing, were dancing jigs of delight. Others were stood on their seats. One or two were even crying. For me, that was the Kop's real Last Stand. The night games were always the best.

Given that we'd seen so many glorious triumphs as Liverpool supporters, celebrating a 3-3 draw was seen by some as a barometer of how our standards had slipped. It wasn't about drawing a game with Man United though. This was about the Kop.

This was a night of pride. A night of passion. A night of defiance. A night when a red and white Kop proved that it could still create the most inspirational, ear-splitting, partisan racket anywhere in football. A night when a point was proven beyond doubt to our visitors.

You might be the biggest club in England.

You might be the darlings of the media.

You might be embarking on an era of success that could one day threaten our own.

You might beat us on the pitch every time you play us but you never have, and never will, come close to creating an atmosphere that beats us off it.

No-one will. Ever.

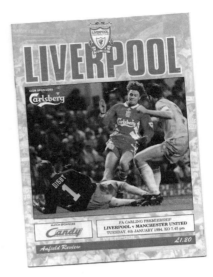

The Kop were unbelievable to me right from my first pre-season game against Newcastle. My abiding memory is of my official Liverpool debut against Sheffield Wednesday and running out in front of 44,000 people who generated so much noise - most of it from the Kop.

It was good to know they were on your side.

The Kop has been packed week in, week out, and the people on it have helped Liverpool win so many games over the years.

My dad used to be amazed by the consistency of those supporters.

Whenever you came to Anfield as an opponent you'd find them getting right behind Liverpool and making things very difficult for the away side.

The Kop was intimidating, not in a nasty way, but by its level of support for the home side.

It made Anfield like a fortress and that meant getting a point was deemed as a great result.

The 3-3 draw between Liverpool and Manchester United was the best game I've ever played in.

I'm not from Merseyside or Manchester but it was impossible not to feel the passion among the supporters.

I'd not experienced anything like that atmosphere at club or international level.

As soon as I saw the flags and banners waving on the Kop, I sensed the night would be special.

I couldn't have been more right and I can honestly say I was privileged.

NIGEL CLOUGH
Former Liverpool striker

'It was the first time I felt I belonged. I was buzzing'

Having stood on the Kop and gone on to captain Liverpool, it's hard to find the right words to describe what it means to me. You could go into superlatives about it.

When I was 11 my mum got some free tickets for the front row of the Kemlyn Road stand for the Inter Milan game. I'd heard all about the Kop because my mum had brought us up as good Liverpudlians.

My love affair with the Kop probably started that night. I watched the Kop more than I did the actual game! The Kop back then was cast in the Liverpool mould. There are so many witty people in this city. There were always jokes on the Kop and they were always original and unique.

You don't like to say it but the Kop influenced more referees than I care to remember in penalty decisions. People say it was Bill Shankly's arrival in 1959 which set Liverpool on the road to success. It was, but it was the part he played with the Kop which was the key.

Everybody wishes they could have gone on to play for Liverpool. The great thing that happened to me was that I was able to play in front of the Kop. It was an unbelievable feeling every time I stepped on to the field.

That feeling of being admired by the people on the Kop is magnificent. From the first time they shout your name you automatically hold them in high regard.

I remember playing in midfield against Leeds when we won the championship in 1972/73.

I was only 19 and Bill Shankly picked me ahead of Brian Hall at the time.

I was just an up and coming young lad and I'd played quite well the week before. I was in the side and I like to think I was in on merit.

Shanks had picked me and I thought to myself 'marvellous'. It was a great occasion. We stayed in a hotel overnight and I remember coming to the game along Anfield Road and I had butterflies.

To settle myself down I started singing to myself on the coach. I was sat there by the window and I started singing 'You'll Never Walk Alone'.

It sounds daft and everything but the passion was burning so much inside me. I was nearly crying.

I'm looking out and thinking 'they're all looking at me here' and I was singing it. It gave me a great buzz and great belief to go into the game.

We played magnificently on the day and I was bursting with desire and pride. We won the game 2-0 which was magnificent. I had a fabulous game and I was so pleased to be part of that team at that time.

During the game it was all going off and I can remember going right through a tackle on Alan Clarke. I really did. It was a block tackle and I went right through and carried on.

I can remember the Kop, mid-game, started to shout my name. They broke out in song and shouted my name.

Hearing them do that so early in my career was tremendous. I was limited as a midfield player but they understood the passion I had.

They didn't chant players' names often during a game. It's something that has to be earned, but that day I felt I'd arrived.

You don't hear things often in a game when you're playing but believe me, I heard that.

It was the first time I felt I belonged. I was buzzing and I'll never forget it. ▶

I was 19 and at a very impressionable age. I always remembered where my brother, Owen, used to stand on the Kop. I used to stand there myself.

So when I'd come out on to the pitch everyone would have their names sung. I was thrilled they were shouting my name but I used to save a special wave for Owen. I knew where he stood and I'd look at him and give him a wave and then he'd give me a wave back.

The lads used to say to me 'how the hell can you see your brother. He's in amongst 26,000 people'. I'd say back: 'I know where I stood and I can look at my brother and pick him out'. I think any supporters throughout the country who stood on their own terrace would know where they stood and if their brother was there. There was also a sporting side to the Kop and that comes with the knowledge of football.

A lot of other supporters would want to lynch opponents if they won but the Kop would give them a

standing ovation if they'd won. You think back to the game when Leeds won the title at Anfield in 1969.

Those Leeds players treasure the memories of being applauded off by the Kop because not many people experience that.

The Kop also showed compassion in the terrible time after Hillsborough.

I know flowers and wreaths were laid at the other end by opponents but people came to Anfield to pay homage to the Kop.

It was as if everyone who died at Hillsborough was a Kopite.

Not all of them stood on the Kop. Many were from other parts of the ground but in the days that passed after Hillsborough everything centred around the Kop. It became a shrine to those who had died.

Anfield was full of scarves, flags and flowers in the goalmouth and everywhere. Those 96 people will never be forgotten. They are as much a part of the Kop folklore as the games against Inter Milan and St Etienne.

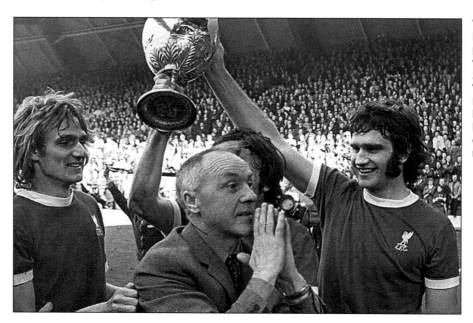

Thanks giving: Bill Shankly prays before the Kop in 1973 as Phil Thompson and Larry Lloyd look on, the league championship raised aloft

Hero worship: A rare archive picture of Liverpool skipper and Shankly's 'Colossus' Ron Yeats, being mobbed by the Kop

We drew with Honved 0-0 in Hungary and Bill Shankly said we could all go out for a drink after such a good result.

We went to a club - probably the only one in Budapest in those days - and the lads pushed me on to the end of a dancing troupe.

When we flew back home I told my family we'd had a quiet time...then television showed the pictures and there I was on screen kicking up my legs. Was I in trouble!

The Kop lads had seen those pictures too and sang at our next home game 'Rowdy does the twist!' The whole ground followed suit in song and I went the colour of my shirt. It was a great experience to play before the Kop and those fans warmed to everybody, friend or foe, who gave 100%.

**RON YEATS,
Former Liverpool skipper**

We were awarded a penalty when we played for Arsenal and I picked up the ball at the Kop end and held one finger up to signify that I was about to put my team one goal in front. It was 0-0 at the time.

I scored but thought about that gesture later on. Can you imagine the flak the Kop would have given me if I'd missed?

I was a former Everton player but the Kop showed respect to players who put in their full lot and I believe I had their vote.

They were wonderful people to play in front of and their power always turned me on.

I believe that I had to match the passion which they showed under that roof. Nothing less would have done for them.

**ALAN BALL
Ex-Everton, Arsenal and England star**

And the band played on: It wasn't often that you got an orchestra on the Kop but a concert took place on the famous terrace in 1994 to mark its Last Stand

'Spion Kop End. Home supporters only. But the spirit lives on'

Those precious 16,480 terrace tickets, admitting fans to a very special Anfield farewell party, unwittingly said it all: Home supporters only. SPION KOP END.

The end it was. But only of an era. The demolition men can break concrete and metal . . .but they can't destroy the spirit of the Kop.

I took my place for the 'Last Stand' on that famous mound as a salute to former Echo sports editor Ernest Edwards - the man who earlier in the century gave the Spion Kop its name. The Liverpool Echo has had a special affinity with the fans at the grassroots ever since.

The turnstiles opened at 1pm and within minutes the central area of the Kop was a sea of red.

One banner bade a nostalgic farewell in a dozen languages (those Scousers are well travelled people). Another carried the simple words: 'Kop's Last Stand - 1906 -1994'.

The Kopites continued to pour in, greeting each other with the warmth of old pals meeting at a celebration party. They immediately made their way to their own personal two square feet of terracing, joining in with the singing and chanting en route.

This was no wake. It was an up-beat and defiant affair. The pitch was bathed in light, but there was suddenly a total eclipse of the sun as a legendary banner swept past. 'Joey Ate The Frogs Legs, Made The Swiss Roll - Now He's Munching Gladbach!'

Yes, a day for stirring great memories and the carnival was now in full swing. At 2.40pm a host of former Kop heroes were introduced to the crowd, including Albert Stubbins, Ian Callaghan, Tommy Smith, Steve Heighway and Phil Thompson.

Two names in particular inspired roars so ear-splitting, they threatened to shatter the glass in the executive boxes. Billy Liddell and Kenny Dalglish

basked in this very special salute.

And then there was Nessie and Jessie.

When Joe Fagan - a great coach and manager in his own right - led out the wives of the legendary Bill Shankly and Bob Paisley, Anfield simply exploded.

"Shankly, Shankly, Shankly," bellowed the Kop as it paid homage to the man who built a Red Empire. The pace of the proceedings meant that Bob didn't get the same treatment, but he still reigns supreme as the most successful English manager of all time.

They've got the Shankly Gates and the Paisley Lounge. Maybe the 'Shankly and Paisley New Kop' is not a bad thought either.

By now the fans were in full flight. They attempted and failed to match their Sixties counterparts with a rendition of "She Loves You," but it got better as the afternoon wore on. The famous Beatles song might now be re-introduced into the Kop's repertoire.

But these memories of great days and super heroes only seemed to emphasise the failings of the present side. The Kop won the day - the players didn't.

Emotion did not prevent straight talking on the terraces. "Three of the back four shouldn't be wearing that famous red jersey. The midfield are all sideways and backwards. There is no quality service whatsoever to the front two (We'd Walk A Million Miles For One Of Your

One more time: The legendary European banner made one last appearance on an emotional day in 1994

Goals, Oh Kenny!)".

Behind me, a lad was rounded on by a girl companion who battered him verbally - and technically - on the question of wingers.

"We haven't got any," said the lad. "You can't expect full-backs to take defenders on. They haven't got the pace or the skill."

"They're supposed to be footballers, aren't they?" rapped the girl. "Just because you're a full-back doesn't mean you can't move wide to give someone an angle". ▶

▶ This vaguely technical retort from a female totally flummoxed the previously dominant male. "Yeh, well they're all useless," he said, returning to basics. "Seven or eight can go next season, no danger".

An older man behind, listening to this exchange, had the last word. "Let's just hope half of them swap shirts with the Norwich players at the end and then get back on the bus to East Anglia by mistake!"

Kopites are steeped in tradition, but they haven't got their heads in the clouds.

At half-time, the humour returned. As one exhausted fan went to sit down on the terrace another told him, tongue in cheek: "Hey, NO seats!"

Behind us we could suddenly hear the sound of lump hammer hitting chisel, striking concrete. Someone was determined to take home his little bit of history.

On the final whistle the revelry subsided as the reality hit home that the Kop's Last Stand was finally over.

Hundreds dallied, reluctant to leave, and there was one final moment of theatre. The players had failed to score, despite chants of: "Play your hearts out for the Kop".

Fittingly, the last goal to be scored at that end was slotted home . . . by a Kopite!

Dressed in long khaki shorts and wearing a false moustache and a red fez, he pushed behind the ring of yellow-jacketed police and placed the ball on the edge of the box.

Roared on, he made an exaggerated dribble towards the goal and then punched the air as his shot found the target.

He was led away and the remaining Kopites drifted away, but the ghost of glories past remained.

As one banner said: 'The Spirit Lives On'.

The last goal: Kopite John Garner, dressed in long khaki shorts and wearing a false moustache and red fez, is led away after scoring in front of the standing Kop for the last time

Anfield goldmine: 10-year-old Robert Dunn from Fazakerley and Liverpool Echo sports editor Ken Rogers with a time capsule that was planted under the old terrace in 1994

'Capsule under the Kop'

Almost two months after the Kop stood for the last time, I would play one final part in the history of this legendary bank of terracing when I presented a 'Time Capsule' to the club on behalf of the Liverpudlian readers of the Echo.

In it was a 'Kop Roll Of Honour' containing the names of thousands of Kopites who had proudly sent their names to the Echo.

A number of items were enclosed in an indestructible box and handed to the man who was Liverpool's chief executive at that time, the famous Peter Robinson. The contents included:

* My own Kop ticket, used to gain entry for the Last Stand against Norwich City from where I reported the game.
* The matchday programme from that day.

* A song sheet used during the special Sunday Kop Concert attended by a host of players and stars.
* A Football Echo and Echo Kop special edition - between them capturing the history of the Kop.
* A Kop video.
* All the players' autographs from the final day.

Bill Pemberton, vice-chairman of the Hillsborough Family Support Group, was kind enough to donate his membership card - number one - and a scarf which was carried by a fan all over Europe as well as on the Kop.

Liverpool FC placed the Time Capsule in the concrete under what became the new Kop Concourse running below the redeveloped stand.

The spot was subsequently marked with a brass plaque, carrying the inscription: 'Liverpool Echo Kop, saluting the fans who made Liverpool great'.

'I'll never **forget** climbing to **the top** of those steps and **looking out** over the glorious Anfield pitch'

The last home game of the 1992-93 season wouldn't seem to be one that would stand out in many Liverpudlians' minds.

Under Graeme Souness it was becoming clear the Reds weren't really going anywhere as we embarked on the '90s - a period when our dominance of the English game would seep away.

But for some reason the match against Spurs seemed special.

It might be that every game in the old Kop was special, with prices far more reasonable and the atmosphere brilliant for virtually every match.

It might be that we were playing a Cockney team - and we always loved to get one over on the Fwanks and Arfurs.

Or it might just be that it was the last home game of the season and a chance to celebrate the fact that we were still the best fans in the country, even if it had been a very mediocre season by Liverpool's standards.

Whatever the reason, it seemed vital to get to Anfield as soon as possible and join the queue on Walton Breck Road to ensure you got in in time to guarantee you didn't miss a minute of the festivities.

So there we were, me, my mate Catty and my brother Kevin, having got the train over from Wirral and in the queue at 10am. Remarkably we weren't the first there, but the three-and-a-half hour wait for the Kop gates to open seemed to fly by.

Whether it was us taking it in turns to nip off to the local shops to get supplies, or whether it was carefully watching the mouth of the mounted policemen's horses to make sure the hanging drool didn't end up being shaken your way, 10am soon became 1pm.

Soon after you could hear the turnstile operators setting up and in the hustle and bustle of trying to make sure no scallies could jump the queue and the policemen shouting to make sure order was kept, you were swept into the ground and up the steps to the back of the Kop.

Treasured memento: Another season on and the standing Kop would be no more

For as long as I live I'll always remember the overwhelming feeling I got whenever I reached the top of those steps and looked out over the gloriously perfect Anfield pitch.

Perhaps every football fan feels the same when they turn up at the ground they love, but to me there was no experience like gaining that first glimpse of my Red place of worship. ▶

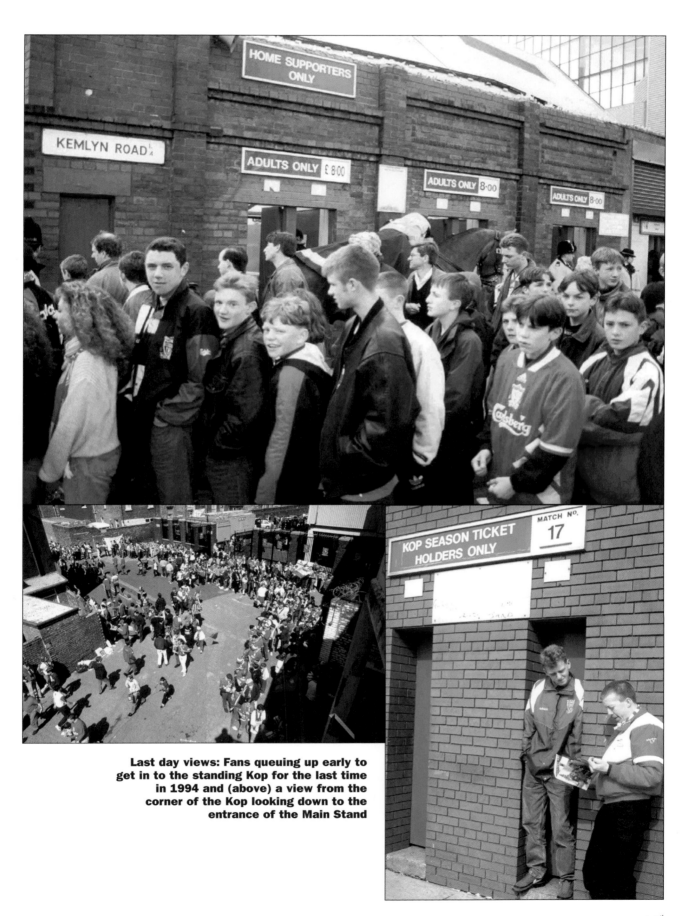

Last day views: Fans queuing up early to
get in to the standing Kop for the last time
in 1994 and (above) a view from the
corner of the Kop looking down to the
entrance of the Main Stand

Like every Kopite it was then a case of making my way to my usual spot which was just behind the right hand goalpost, about 15 rows up on the new Kop.

At first you could sit down to rest your feet after hours of standing up, but within half an hour you had to get up to protect your patch, which for us was just behind a bar, next to a pillar.

The first action on the pitch came when the Spurs players stepped out of the tunnel in their suits to soak up the atmosphere on the brilliantly sunny day.

There were real boos - not the token effort you get these days when the opposition team is read out - and the likes of Teddy Sheringham, Ian Walker and Vinny Sideways stood on the halfway line with their programmes, looking calm but intimidated by the wall of sound they were greeted by.

As they milled around, captain Gary Mabbutt obviously felt he would strike a blow for his side by wandering on his own towards the Kop goal, in a show of defiance.

How dare he strut his stuff on our turf! We shouted abuse and blasted out all the Cockney chants we knew, and hoped he would be made to pay for his insolence by the misfiring Reds when the game got underway

The only other thing I recall, apart from the incredible repertoire of chants and songs that you just don't get before games these days, and the Kop being

full an hour before kick-off, was the balloon that floated around on the pitch.

It seemed to come from nowhere and descended to ground near the halfway line.

It made its way towards the Kop goal and we all went 'oooooooohhhhhh', then a gust of wind would sweep it off course and there would be boos. Then it headed towards the Kop again before ending up in the net and the cheer was as loud as if Torben Piechnik had had his contract terminated.

By kick-off the Kop were well up for the game, even though there was little more at stake than pride. Fortunately for the atmosphere on the day, there is a lot of pride among Reds fans and the noise was as if the match was a title decider.

But as exciting and compelling as the atmosphere was, standing behind our bar was becoming a struggle as the Kop swayed and the weight of hundreds of fans seemed to be directed towards us. As much as I wanted the Reds to win, part of me wanted the game to end 0-0 as I knew a surge of delirious Kopites could make me pass out. The game ended 6-2!

Fortunately, during the celebration of the first goal, we were able to duck under the bar and find a space where we could enjoy the rest of the entertainment in more comfort. It was important to soak up every

morsel of action as a long summer without football lay ahead. Thrashing Cockneys is always fun but after a season of disappointment a goal feast gave hope - false hope as it turned out - for the future and the three hours or so of almost non-stop singing made the entertaining game merely a bonus on a superb day.

In those days being a Kopite on a match day was a day-long experience.

You couldn't stroll up five minutes before kick-off with a premium view seat waiting for you.

The best things come to those who wait and anyone who was mad enough to queue up with us from 10am for a top Kop spec that day will vouch for that.

'Heaven was a 68 bus ride to the Kop'

Heaven was just a No 68 bus ride to the Kop. The 68 bus from Bootle to Stanley Park was full to capacity and it was match day at Anfield. I was seven years old and in the charge of my elder brother Malcolm. He was about to introduce me to the Kop.

Excited? I couldn't hide it. Like everybody else aboard, I was gripped by the passion, the atmosphere and the expectancy. I had never been to Anfield before.

I was decked out in red, of course, and I carried a heavy wooden rattle which would be classed as a dangerous object in 1994.

Once inside the boys' pen, I remember staring in bewilderment at the thousands who congregated under that famous roof.

Their feelings for Liverpool were ultimate and their humour was unbeatable. The best. I joined the Red Army that day.

That was my beginning and I'm sure that every Kopite will have his own similar story to tell.

There was the place where we stood too . . . a little piece of concrete, we felt, was our own personal property. I still look at the spot which was mine.

Then came Bill Shankly and the greatest of all manager-supporter relationships began. It will never be equalled. The common bond and honest expression was unique.

Fans and manager were inseparable. After today, of course, the old Kop will disappear and the new all-seater stand will be erected.

The bricks and mortar will be different, but the people will remain the same. They have been the heartbeat of this club and vital to its marvellous achievements.

The volume of the Kop will be turned up to maximum whenever 100 percent is given on the pitch. It has always been that way.

Meanwhile, we welcome Norwich City on this extra special day and the players are eager to sign off the season in style.

Football cannot be stage-managed but we will be aiming for an open thrilling game. Fortunately, our visitors also have a reputation for interesting and attacking football. I hope to see a performance which is fitting on this memorable occasion.

Finally, it is my duty on behalf of the club to thank everybody for their wonderful support this season.

**ROY EVANS
(Programme notes from The Kop's Last Stand v Norwich City, April 30, 1994)**

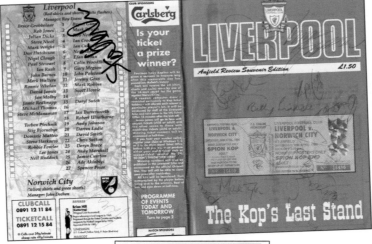

The last word: The manager's notes and an autographed cover of the 'Last Stand' programme

And You'll Never Walk Alone: Former Liverpool boss Roy Evans joins Gerry Marsden and former players Tommy Smith and Alan Hansen in an emotional rendition of the famous anthem in 1994. Above: A side view of the Kop in its last standing season

The generation game: Billy O'Donnell (far left) the loyal Kopite who stood on the old terracing for the last time in 1994 after watching the Reds since the 1920s. Above: Young fans on the standing Kop for the last time. Left: The 1993-4 squad and (below) an early view from the new Kop stand

'Demolishing the Kop

I started work on the demolition of the Spion Kop after the Norwich game. I was the works manager for McAlpine Fusiliers on there and worked right through the demolition of the old Kop and the building of the new one right up to its completion.

I was actually the assistant works manager on the Centenary Stand when that was built a few years earlier and also worked on the Stretford End at Manchester United before working on the Kop.

I'm a lifelong Liverpool fan and I stood on the Kop watching the great teams right through. I started going there as a kid in about 1965.

I went with my father and my granddad. My uncle, Phil Morgan, was a player at the club so we used to get tickets and go to the games nearly every other week. The reserves played at Anfield then so we'd go and watch them and then the first team.

When I was older I'd go with my mates. A big gang of us would thumb it from the lights at Bromborough right through to Anfield.

I've been all over the country and all over Europe watching Liverpool so to go from supporting Liverpool to working on the new Kop was really a dream come true.

Demolishing the Kop gave me mixed emotions. Knocking it down was quite sad but in terms of enjoying my work, in the sense of where I was working, it was excellent. We had a great team of lads working on it, all who were local.

We did all sorts as well as simply building it. We concreted in the time capsule which is under the Kop and we also, at the front apron of the Kop before you go on to the pitch, concreted in some urns of ashes in there.

The groundsman, Reg Summers, allowed people to come on to the pitch and walk around to scatter ashes but because we were concreting in at the time the people asked us if, instead of scattering the ashes, could we bury the casket in the concrete. We buried quite a few in there.

We built the new Kop in four main stages and we

were under quite a lot of pressure.

When Man United rebuilt the Stretford End they closed it down completely while the work was going on. At Liverpool the fans were allowed on to the new stand as each section was built.

There was a time when stadium manager Ged

gave me **mixed** emotions'

**Something missing?
A haunting scene as the old Kop returns
to how it started – an old piece of
wasteland in the north of Liverpool**

**Kop job:
Gary on the
hallowed
turf as the
terrace
comes down**

Poynton and chief executive Peter Robinson said "Listen lads, are we going to have it open for the Newcastle game?"

We had two weeks at that point to get the job done and there was quite a lot of work left to do. We did it though, which was a great achievement.

Here today, gone tomorrow: The Kop's 'Last Stand' and the old terrace in ruins during the summer of '94

'The old terrace's time is up. Can Liverpool be great without it?'

*I*ts corners are known as pulpits, its crash barriers are scored with adorations and its steps wouldn't look out of place outside a cathedral. But on Monday 2 May, worship will cease on THE KOP. Before the bulldozers move in, 90 MINUTES gets all nostalgic about Liverpool's legendary terrace.

The Spion Kop ceases to exist after Liverpool's match against Norwich this Saturday. The celebrated cinder banking that has pulsed with life for 90 years, supporting millions of dockers' boots, winkle-pickers and Reeboks, will be bulldozed into myth. Maybe it's just as well.

"The Kop was full 90 minutes before kick-off," read the match reports after a recent fixture against Newcastle, before describing how the home team were outplayed on their own turf by the visitors.

The terrace has become an anachronistic reminder of Anfield's illustrious past.

On the Sunday immediately following the Norwich game, Liverpool fans will have the chance to pay their final respects at a specially organised 'Kop Party', in which Gerry Marsden and a host of local celebrities and pop stars will provide the entertainment.

Then the demolition men move in.

The new stand, by all accounts, will be a single-tier construction with a capacity of around 12,000. 'By all accounts' because the club are notoriously backward about coming forward.

Like a modern-day Medusa, the receptionist jealously guards all avenues of approach to Peter Robinson, the chief executive.

But then, the more astute Kopites have always recognised the distinction between supporting the club and supporting the team.

Bill Shankly once said: "We created an institution - something more than a football club, something alive and vibrant, and warm and successful."

Times have changed. These days, Hercules would have trouble breaching Anfield's red tape.

Sou this is it: A cartoon on the Kop's last stand, which appeared in 90 Minutes in 1994

But enough about the club.

Back to the Kop, which, as early as 1957, Manchester United boss Matt Busby described as, "Liverpool's most prized possession".

Built in 1906 to coincide with the Reds' second Championship triumph, the Spion Kop was named after a hilltop in South Africa where 300 British soldiers, the majority from Merseyside and Lancashire regiments, lost their lives during the Boer War.

It was extended and roofed in 1928 to accommodate close on 30,000 spectators, making it the largest covered terracing in the country.

It earned its reputation, though, in the '60s.

Shankly was installed, the music scene was swinging and the Kop was swaying.

Among the sea of faces standing on its yawning slopes were future stars like Phil Thompson, Joey Jones and Jimmy Case.

Shankly, too, when the mood took him.

"One night we ran out on the pitch for a European game and we thought the Kop was on fire," recalls former Liverpool striker Ian St John.

"It looked like smoke was bellowing up out of it, but it was steam. It was raining, the fans had all gone in soaked and the heat from all the bodies was drying out their clothes".

The fervour and fanaticism may have been watered down over the years, and fathers may tell sons that it's not the same any more, but the Kop still has over 10,000 season ticket holders and gates at Anfield regularly exceed 40,000 to this day.

More to the point, the hallowed cave has remained a relatively safe place to watch football.

One of the most serious injuries to have occurred there happened when a woman broke her hip when she slipped on one of the greasy blackened steps during a Billy Graham sermon when the American evangelist toured Britain in 1984.

"When I was a player, I was privileged to be cheered on by some 26,000 on the Kop," says former favourite Kevin Keegan, who returned to Anfield in triumph as manager of Newcastle.

"For the current players, it's 16,000 and now it's going to be down to 12,000 when the seats are in.

"For me, Liverpool Football Club nor the ground will ever be the same.

"It was the Kop which made Anfield a special place to play and watch football and I'm terribly sad to see it go".

Modern thinking and safety requirements have rendered the Kop obsolete.

Barring a dramatic intervention by the Heritage Department and the bestowal of listed building status, the old terrace's time is up.

But the question now is: Can Liverpool become great again without it?

36   'We all live in a red-and-white Kop.'

Dawn of a new era: Shafts of sunlight illuminate the new seated Kop stand

'I scored two goals and the Kop were singing 'sign him on! sign him on!"

The one game in front of the Kop that really stands out for me was my last Merseyside derby before I went to Juventus.

I needed two goals against Everton to equal Dixie Dean's record of scoring 19 goals in Merseyside derbies.

At the time everyone knew it was my last season at Liverpool and my last derby game.

I scored a goal in the first half and in the second half we were attacking the Kop end. At the time I didn't know I'd be coming back to Liverpool and the Kop were willing me on to score the second goal.

We were 2-1 up and there was less than 10 minutes left when I scored a second past Neville Southall.

It was great to equal a record like that and I'd say that the Kop made me do it. I still feel now that the crowd played a major part in me equalling that record.

It was incredible after I'd scored. They were just shouting my name over and over again for the next 10 minutes.

I've got a great picture of me scoring that goal and on it you can see one of the stewards, who is meant to keep calm, jumping in the air with the Kop in the background.

I was very lucky to have a good relationship with the Kop supporters.

They're clever people because even if you play badly, as long as they see you put the effort in they realise it and support you.

The first goal I ever scored for Liverpool as a kid was at the Kop end. They gave me a great reception and I looked at that and thought 'I want to score down this end all the time'.

Bob Paisley used to say to us, and I'm sure this came from Bill Shankly originally, that they are worth a goal start.

If we were drawing or losing, and in the second half we were facing the Kop end, it had a major influence on the team. They would get behind us and give us a little but extra.

Another thing Bob used to say, and it was quite amazing really, was that sometimes when it was windy at Anfield you'd stand in the penalty area at the Kop end and it wasn't windy. The wind had somehow suddenly stopped.

I think that was to do with the design of the Kop and the people on it. Mind you, Bob would also say that if the ball was on the goal-line the Kop would suck it into the back of the net!

I remember the night when I played in Alan Hansen's testimonial in 1988.

I was still playing in Italy at the time and I came back to play for Liverpool in a game against an England XI.

I think I scored two goals and the Kop were all shouting my name and 'sign him on, sign him on'. It was incredible.

I was still a Juventus player but that was when I realised that I wanted to come back to Liverpool.

I'd been in Italy for a year but coming back and pulling on a Liverpool shirt was very special to me. But really it was the Kop, and the way they made me feel welcome, which made me want to come back.

My own testimonial night took place in front of the new Kop which wasn't fully finished at the time. It was a superb night for me.

Loads turned up for it and it showed how well I got on with them. It was a special night. We won 6-0 against Celtic and I scored one. ▶

Mutual Appreciation Society: Rushie saluting the Kop and (below) in typical goalscoring form at the Kop end

When we were four or five nil up I hadn't scored and the Kop just wanted me to score. They weren't bothered about the result, they just wanted me to score.

When I did they were just so happy. It was a great occasion.

The Kop's Last Stand against Norwich was another great day. It was a carnival and we were all very aware that it was a day for the people who stood on there.

We found it hard to focus on the game itself and I think that's why we lost 1-0. We were more concerned about playing in front of the legendary stand for the last time and the people on there.

I have to say though I've got no bad memories of the Kop. I'm very lucky and they're memories that can never be taken away from me.

I've got a picture at home of my wife and my two boys, when they were younger, stood in there on the Kop.

My boys wouldn't have really known the Kop as it was then but I keep saying to them 'This is you standing on the famous Kop'.

They can look back at that photo and say they stood on the Kop, like thousands and thousands of others, and that's something you can never take away from them.

'I have to say I've got no bad memories of the Kop. I'm very lucky and they're memories that can never be taken away from me'

All together now: Ian Rush and Robbie Fowler join the fans for a special concert to say farewell to the old Kop in 1994

**A star is born: One of Robbie Fowler's five against Fulham – but it felt like
the beginning of the end for the old Kop**

'A shadow of its former self'

Perhaps the strangest night I spent on the old Spion Kop was the last time I actually stood on it.

It was the night when Robbie Fowler scored five against Fulham in the Coca-Cola Cup in 1993.

We'd won the first leg 3-1 at Craven Cottage and not many could be bothered with the second leg.

Only 12,541 turned up for the game, which was played during the deepest, darkest days under Souness, and I remember thinking that I'd never had so much space to move in on the Kop.

Fulham brought with them about 200 fans, who were sat in the middle of the Lower Centenary, and the atmosphere at kick-off was dire.

You'll Never Walk Alone was murmured so quietly that I began to wonder why I'd bothered going.

The last time I'd heard the Kop so quiet in a cup game was when I watched Marine play Rochdale there in 1989 and the terracing wasn't even open that night.

I'm glad I was there though.

It was a significant night in Fowler's life and I'm still proud to say I've seen every minute of first team football he's ever played at Anfield.

The Toxteth Terror, playing in only his second game at Anfield, scored five goals - most with consummate ease - and made us all realise what a classy kid we had on our hands.

It also made me realise that the Kop was a shadow of it's former self.

There were still a couple of great nights, the last hurrahs, to come before the bulldozers arrived but that night it felt like I had a terminally ill friend who knew his time was up.

'It was very emotional. No-one else in the country does tributes like that'

The mosaics were first suggested by Rick Parry. He was very impressed with what he had seen in places like Milan and Barcelona and came up with the idea.

They can take Andy Knott, who designs and organises them, four to six hours to do.

They are normally done the day before the game and we usually appeal for helpers.

Sometimes you get quite a few come down to help. A lot of school kids have come down and helped out.

There's a lot of legwork involved - running up and down the Kop and making sure they're in the right places. When you've got 70 steps it tires you out.

The club pay for the mosaics. It's not a whim of the crowd, they're sponsored by the club.

We did the first one against Manchester United but the next one against Sheffield Wednesday drew a lot of attention.

On previous seasons we had been to Sheffield and been treated like dirt.

They wouldn't let Liverpool fans take floral tributes into the ground because they were ridiculously seen as 'a danger'. People were told they couldn't even take single roses in to put in the Leppings Lane end.

Instead they put tables, the sort of thing you'd see at car boot sales, outside the ground to put the flowers on.

They also put a statement out saying they wouldn't put a plaque or memorial up as it would be seen as a sign of guilt.

So when Sheffield Wednesday came to Anfield we organised a mosaic on the Kop, consisting of red cards, which was aimed at the Sheffield Wednesday directors.

When they saw it, it stunned them. They could not believe the strength of feeling.

It was a tribute to the people who had died at Hillsborough and a statement that we wanted Sheffield Wednesday to erect a memorial in a suitable place.

There's now a memorial there - we like to think that one worked.

Two others which stand out are the Shankly day and Paisley night.

Bob's wife, Jessie, came out on to the pitch on the Paisley night.

The following day she rang me up and wanted to thank me for organising it.

I told her that was the wrong way round, it was us me who wanted to thank her, but she sent me a tenner through the post for some fanzines!

I couldn't believe it. I sent it back. That just shows the person she is.

The Shankly day, against Coventry in 1999, probably meant the most to me. That was incredible. The mosaic was a picture of Shankly that day.

After the game there were parties across the city. It was a fantastic celebration.

The most famous mosaics are probably the 'GH' one and the 'Allez, Allez' one from the 2001/02 season.

They were incredible. The 'GH' one was at the Manchester United game, just after he had been taken ill.

It wasn't deliberately aimed at the United game, it just fell that way, and Gerard later said he saw it on the television.

The 'Allez, Allez' one was for the Roma game, Gerard's homecoming, and it was a very emotional night.

No-one else in this country does tributes ▶

Back to the future: Mosaics have been a popular way of keeping the seated Kop's spirit alive. A Hillsborough '96' mosaic (above) and (left) a You'll Never Walk Alone mosaic from the final game of the 2001-2002 season against Ipswich

◆ like that.

We've tried very hard to let the past live on and keep it going. We've tried to keep the Kop unique.

Looking back, St Etienne was an amazing night. There were all those French fans in the Anfield Road end and people had never seen those vast numbers of away fans in Europe before, apart from when Celtic came down in 1966.

That was the night where the 'Allez, Allez' came from. It was a great night but for me the best night at Anfield was the Roma night.

That's because of the whole emotion of the occasion and that night we were playing against a team who were possibly the best in the whole of Europe.

They were a very, very good side and full of star names. Against St Etienne, to be honest, we all thought we'd win.

I'm not sure we did against Roma because they'd also won at Anfield 12 months previously.

We won 2-0 and I just think that night was something really, really special.

If that was the Kop's swansong then I'd be happy with that.

'We've tried very hard to let the past live on and keep it going. We've tried to keep the Kop unique'

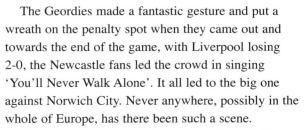
'Going out with a bang!'

The first flag day was against Spurs on the last day of the 1992/93 season. A Liverpool supporter by the name of John Mackin was the brains behind it.

The Gwladys Street had become seated at Everton and that was worthy of just a few lines in the Echo.

The Stretford End at Old Trafford had been seated and again went with a whimper. It didn't go out with a bang. There wasn't even a slight smouldering of anything.

It was the same everywhere. Everyone was closing their terraces and going out in grand silences.

That couldn't happen on the Kop. You couldn't let all that history, all that singing, chanting, flag waving and unique goal celebrations go without making a statement.

It was never a protest about seats being put in. It was a statement of the Kop's strength as a body of people.

The club never stood in the way, nor did the Police.

The BBC covered the game but more or less ignored it. Towards the end of the game, which we won 6-2, they did say the Kop were having a carnival and that's exactly what it was.

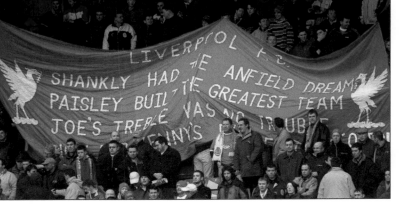

It was a celebration of what was a dry run for the Kop's last day the following season.

There were about 16,000 on the Kop that day and it was estimated there were 3,000-4,000 flags.

The next flag day was the 3-3 draw with Manchester United which was again a fantastic night.

The Manchester Evening News and even Alex Ferguson praised the Kop that night.

He said at the time he'd never seen anything like it.

The next one was against Newcastle which coincided with the 5th anniversary of Hillsborough.

The Geordies made a fantastic gesture and put a wreath on the penalty spot when they came out and towards the end of the game, with Liverpool losing 2-0, the Newcastle fans led the crowd in singing 'You'll Never Walk Alone'. It all led to the big one against Norwich City. Never anywhere, possibly in the whole of Europe, has there been such a scene.

There were queues round the ground from half past ten in the morning. The number of flags and banners on the Kop that day must have numbered around 5,000.

There were '60s scarves, Juve flags, Roma flags, flags from '77, the Joey Jones banner, the Shankly remembrance one, the Shankly lives forever one and the one that was the most amazing of them all - 'The Spirit of The Kop Lives On'.

Anybody who was there will never forget that day. People went and sat in the Anfield Road end just so they could take photos of the Kop.

The humour was incredible. I remember a chant of 'you're supposed to let us win' went round when we went 1-0 down.

45 minutes after the game the Kop was still half-full with people refusing to go home.

People were lying down and sleeping. There was even a guy with a fez who ran on to the pitch just because he wanted to be the last person to ever score at the Kop end.

It was something that has never been seen before or since. It was a tribute to the history of what had gone before. The Kop couldn't disappear off the face of football without there being something there to remember it by.

It showed what the Kop was all about.

'The St Etienne of a

Roma 2002. Gerard Houllier's return. Rightly regarded as the greatest night the all-seater Kop has seen.

Before the game Phil Thompson had said it could be St Etienne part two. Afterwards it felt like it was. It was certainly the St Etienne of a new generation and one hell of a night.

For me though, it was somewhat bittersweet because I wasn't on the Kop. I was in the Anfield press box, working for the Liverpool Echo, and didn't quite feel as part of the night as I could have.

I was on the Kop for the Paris St Germain game in 1997, right up in the back corner. The noise that night was sensational. Liverpool didn't quite do enough to go through but the PSG players, many of them internationals, were visibly frightened by the atmosphere.

My throat was on fire by full-time. It was a night of glorious failure and one that I'd felt very much part of. It's not the same when you're working.

The hardest part of watching the club you love and support from a press box is suppressing your emotions. Singing, chanting and celebrating goals isn't the done thing in the press box. You're there to cover the game, not lead the singing.

So whenever I've been sat in the press box and Liverpool have scored it's been a case of sitting there and simply watching the celebrations unfold around me. It's bloody hard.

Remember the 2001 FA Cup Final when Michael Owen scored his superb late winner? While you were going bananas and hugging the nearest person in sight, I was sat in the Millennium Stadium's press box describing the goal down the phone for the Football Echo.

My immediate thought was how I was going to describe the goal for my report, which had to be

A night to remember: Gerard Houllier shows his delight after the memorable 2-0 win over Roma, thanks to goals from Jari Litmanen and Emile Heskey – and, of course, the power of the Kop, opposite page

new generation'

finished and ready to print at full-time, rather than enjoying what in reality is the greatest moment I've ever experienced inside a football ground.

Don't get me wrong, I wouldn't swap working as a football writer for the world and I am very privileged to be doing it, but being professional under those circumstances isn't easy.

The Roma night was similar. We'd heard strong whispers that Gerard would make his long awaited return that night and on arrival at Anfield I was told that he was definitely there.

The noise when he walked out of the tunnel again was superb but with the scrum of cameramen around him, and Fabio Cappello, only the people in the Paddock and Main Stand could really see him.

Early in the first half he came to the touchline to pass instructions on and everyone on the Kop saw him.

The noise was phenomenal. 'Allez, Allez, Gerard

Houllier' rang around Anfield like never before. It was one of those goosepimple moments that I'll never forget.

With a noise like that against them, Roma, who were the Italian champions at the time and one of the favourites to win the Champions League outright, didn't stand a chance.

Liverpool secured the 2-0 win they needed to go through to the quarter-finals thanks to a penalty from Jari Litmanen and a header from Emile Heskey.

In one sense it was good to sit there and experience the atmosphere, watching well-known members of the national press constantly gaze towards the Kop because they couldn't help it.

But on the other hand it would have been great to have been right in the centre of it all on the Kop for what, arguably, could be Anfield's last truly great European night.

THE FIELDS OF ANFIELD ROAD

Outside the Shankly Gates,
I heard a Kopite calling.
Shankly they have taken you away,
But you left a great eleven,
Before you went to heaven,
Now it's glory round the Fields of Anfield Road.

All round the Fields of Anfield Road,
Where once we watched the King Kenny play (And could he play),
Stevie Heighway on the wing,
We had dreams and songs to sing,
Of the glory round the Fields of Anfield Road.

Outside the Paisley Gates,
I heard a Kopite calling,
Paisley they have taken you away,
You led the great eleven,
Back in Rome in '77,
And the Redmen they're still playing the same way.

A re-write of the Irish folk-song 'Fields of Athenry', Liverpool's most popular
current song was written in the 1995/96 season. Again, the original was slightly
different from the version that is sung now. The first line of the chorus was
originally 'Oh Ohh the Fields of Anfield Road' rather than the 'All round the
fields of Anfield Road' that we all know and sing today. The 'And could he
play' shouted at the end of the second line was only added later and was
originally 'And he could play'. 'Stevie Heighway on the wing' is also sung by
the vast majority now although originally it was written as 'We had Heighway
on the wing'. There's also been a few subtle changes to the first verse over time
while the second verse was only added at a later date.

YOU'LL NEVER WALK ALONE

When you walk through a storm,
Hold your head up high,
And don't be afraid of the dark.
At the end of the storm,
There's a golden sky,
And the sweet silver song of a lark.
Walk on through the wind,
Walk on through the rain,
Though your dreams be tossed and blown.
Walk on, walk on,
With hope in your heart,
And you'll never walk alone,
You'll never walk alone.
Walk on, walk on,
With hope in your heart,
And you'll never walk alone,
You'll never walk alone.

Richard Rodgers and Oscar Hammerstein II wrote the original in 1945 for Broadway musical play Carousel. It has since been covered by a whole host of artists all over the world including; Louis Armstrong, Chet Atkins, Shirley Bassey, Glen Campbell, Ray Charles, Perry Como, Michael Crawford, Placido Domingo, Aretha Franklin, Judy Garland, Marilyn Horne, Mahalia Jackson, Patti LaBelle, Cleo Laine, Mario Lanza, Darlene Love, Jim Nabors, Olivia Newton John, Pink Floyd, Elvis Presley, The Righteous Brothers, Nina Simone, Frank Sinatra, Kiri Te Kanawa, Conway Twitty and Dionne Warwick. But it was the version that Gerry and the Pacemakers released in October '63 that the Kop took as their own and subsequently became the anthem of Liverpool Football Club. In 1985 a recording of the song by pop and rock stars was released to raise money for the victims of the Bradford City fire disaster when 56 supporters lost their lives and almost 300 were injured after a fire at Valley Parade. The song stayed at number one in the charts for most of the summer and hundreds of thousands of pounds were raised.

It's the off-the-cuff chants, the funny one liners that have made the Kop stand out from other crowds over the years. The Kop's sense of humour is unique. The hilarious and often crude put-downs that have rolled down from the Kop during its hey-day wouldn't be found anywhere else. It's not simply a case of the old 'every Scouser's a comedian' cliché. If that was true then there'd be the same tales to tell from Goodison Park. There aren't. Every ground has witnessed its funny moments but few like the Kop did. Remember these?

Who's Up Mary Brown (to the tune of 'Knees up Mother Brown' and sung to Tommy Docherty after it was revealed he was having an affair with the United physio's wife Mary Brown)

Don't Cry for Me Tina, Tina, (sung to Peter Shilton after an encounter with a woman called Tina)

There's only one Blackpool Tower and What's the weather like up there? (sung to 6ft 7in striker Kevin Francis)

There's only one Freddie Boswell (sung to Liverpool chairman David Moores as he opened the Centenary Stand in 1992)

Alan Ball, Alan Ball, is it true what Shankly says, you'll win f*** all? (sung to Alan Ball after he turned down Liverpool to sign for Everton)

Denis Law, Denis Law is it true what Shankly says, you're sixty-four? (sung to a laughing Denis Law shortly before he retired)

Binman, binman, what's the score? (sung to former Llandudno binman Neville Southall when Liverpool were winning on derby day)

Are you City in disguise? (sung in ironic fashion, as it was originally their chant, to Man United fans during a 3-1 defeat at Anfield in 2001)

Elvis, Elvis, give us a song (sung to Fulham's Elvis Hammond in 2003)

Charlton, Charlton, I'd walk a million miles to the end of your neck, Charlton (sung, to the tune of Al Johnson's 'My Mammy', to Jack Charlton when he played at Anfield for Leeds)

Go back to Italee, go back to Italee and Ee-aye-addio, Mussolini's dead (both sung during Inter Milan '65)

Are you watching Mrs Wark? (after John Wark had been struck in the groin during a match)

One Kevin Scully, there's only one Kevin Scully (sung during the filming of Alan Bleasdale's 'Scully' at half-time in front of the Kop)

Freddie Laker, Freddie Laker, Bruce is better in the air (sung when Bruce Grobbelaar caught a shot in a game shortly after Freddie Laker's Laker Airways went bust owing £270 million in 1982)

Where did you get them boots? (sung to Tommy Smith when he appeared in white boots)

Thank you very much for paying a million, thank you very much, thank you very, very much (sung during Ronnie Whelan's testimonial against Newcastle after Kevin Keegan had paid £1 million for Liverpool keeper Mike Hooper)

The Esso sign means happy motoring . . . (a famous TV advert in the '60s, it was sung when Petrolul Ploesti, a team from the Romanian oil country, walked out on to the Anfield pitch in 1966)

What a waste of money (sung to inspirational free transfer signing Gary McAllister during his last game for Liverpool)

Kop Scroll Of Honour

Keith Richard Abraham
Gordon A Ackers
Chester John Adams
Alan Adlington
Tony Ainsworth
Reyhan Akkurt
Christopher Allen
Peter Allen
Paul Allman
Ken Alman
Michael Anderson
Ray Annal
Wayne Appleton
Mike Arends
Ally Arkwright
Teresa Armitage
Jason Armshaw
Brian Ashcroft
Neal Ashcroft
Kenneth Ashun
Lauren Ashun
Lee Ashun
David W Ashworth
Ian C Ashworth
Fred Askew
Marc Robert Astick
Ste Astley
Michael Austin
Dennis Baccino
Charles Bagley
Chris 'RID' Bailey
John Baker
Stephen D Ball
Kevin Ball
Derek Bardwa
Mr Frank Barker
Austin Barrett
Alec Barrow
James William Bates
Brian Stanley Beacall
Graeme Beacall
Steven Beacom
Neil Beardwood
Ronald Beatie
Frank Beckett
Richard Beech
Alan Bell
Mark Bell
Carmel Bennett
Sian Ann Bennett
Alan Bennion
Michael Bennion

George Bibbey
Harold 'Adge' Bibbey
Dean Bicknell
Ross Bicknell
Darren Biddlestone
Neil Bigelow
John Bills
Gordon Birch
Leslie Birch
Richard Black
Kevin Blackburne
Gwilym Blackwell
Karl Gerhard Blain
James Blair
Ronnie Blaylock
Dave Blinston
John Blundell
Kevin Boardman
Tom Bogan
Joe Boon
William Henry Booth
Pauline Booth
Michael Bowman
Tom Boycott
Matthew Boyd
Steve Boyes
Ciaran Boyle
Jimmy Boyle
Gerard Bradley
Michael Bradley
William 'Eddie' Bradshaw
Ann Breadner
Lee James Breadner
Jack Brent
N Brogan
Christopher Bromilow
Michaela Bromilow
Raymond Bromley
Ben York Brooks
Stephen Anthony Brooks
Phil Brough
Christopher Brown
Kevin Brown
Lee Brown
Simon Brown
James Robert Bryan
Hugh Bryce
Amy Louise Burge
Donald Burns
Mike Burrows
Barry Burton
Damian Burton

Paul Christopher Byrne
Denis V Byrne
Dennis Cain
Stuart Malcolm Caine
John Cairns
Mel Cairns
Alan Campbell
Neil Campbell
Reg Carmichael
Ken Carr
Adam Carroll
Alan Carter
Alan Carter
Alan Samuel Carter
Alan Edward Carter
David Mark Carter
Ellanor Carter
John William Carter
Peter Carter
Chris Carver
Betty Case
Gerry Casey
William Caton
Peter Cave
Alan Cessford
Michelle Louise Chandler
Gerry Chapple
Kev Chapple
Mike Chapple
Les Cheeseman
Roy Cheetham
Mr Leslie Clark
Paul Clarke
Steven Clarke
John Clinton
Jamie Clynch
Andy Cochrane
Keith Coker
David Colleran
Liz Collingwood
Joe Collins
Raymond Collins
Alan Charles Coman
Josh Condell
Michael Connell
Joe Connolly
Lee Connor
Simon Connor
Alan Constantine
Kevin Cooney
Justin Cooney
Steve Corbett

Brian C Cosgrove
Alan Cottrell
Stephen Coughlan
Matthew Cowen
Billy Cox
Laura Crabb
Chris Crawford
Paul Creamer
Andrew Cribb
Thomas Crowe
Terry Culligan
John Keith Cundy
David Curran
Mark Currie
Tony Curtis
AndreW Cushion
John Dacey
Colin Daly
Sean Paul Daniels
Stephen Daulby
Ben Paul Lee Davies
Fiona Davies
John Martin Davies
Louise G Davies
Mark Davies
Michael Davies
Peter Davies
Sid 'Ooch' Davies
William F Davies
Ron Dawson
Carlo De Martini
Jack Deane
Ernie Dempster
Robert Denby
Paul Dennis
Mark Devereaux
Stephen Devine
George Devonport
Ronnie C Dewhurst
Mark Dickinson
Kiri Dickson
Paul Disley
Alan Dixon
Kevin Dixon
John A Dobson
J Eric Doig
Roy Dollin
Scott Donegan
Brian Donnellan
Chas Donnelly
James Dixie Donnelly
John Donnelly
Michael Donnelly
Stephen Donnelly
Rob Dolphin
Kevin Dooley

Allan Doran
Alan 'Dare' Douglas
Alex Dove
Paul Dove
Sean Dove
Alexander Dowbiggin
William Dowling
Mrs Blodwen Doyle
Liam Doyle
Kevan Draper
Neil Dring
Iain Duff
Alan Duffy
Kevin James Dunn
Tomas Dunn
Simon Dunne
Owen Dutton
Martin Easthope
Ian Eccles
Stephen Eccles
Carl Eden
Jimmy Eden
Kristian R Edvartsen
Kate Edwards
Sian Edwards
Steven Edwards
Mr Trevor Edwards
Brian Ellis
Edith Ellis
Liam Ennis
Stephen Ennis
John Enwright
Gareth John Evans
James Evans
John Evans
Owen Evans
James Fagan
Thomas George Fagan
Tommy Fairky
Rodney Fallon
Sahra Farah
Mrs Faughn
Gary Faulkner
Martin Fazal
T J Fearon
Alan Feeney
Andrew Ference
John Fewtrell
Craig Finn
Jason Firth
Roy Firth
John J Flaherty
Kevin P Flaherty
Stephen Flanagan
Luke Thomas Flannery
Michael Flatley

Joseph Fleetwood
Danny Fleming
Edward Fleming
Mike Flockhart
Richard Foley
John Forsyth
Angela Foxley
Graham Foxley
Liam Freeburn
Charles Gallagher
W Harry Games
Lee Gannon
Basil Gannon
Dave Garbutt
James Gardiner
Brian Garner
Roy Gates
Craig Brian Gaughan
David George
Peter Anthony Gibney
Pop Gibney
Michael Gibson
Kenny Giles
Gary William Gilsenan
Colin Gilvin
Ken Goddard
Ian Gordon
Paul Gosling
Robert Gough
David William Gould
Christine Grace
Peter Grace
John Graham
William Joseph Graham
Jack 'Australia' Grant
Ernie Green
Janice Green
Sandy Greene
Damon Greenhalgh
Sian Greenway
Anthony Greenwood
Christopher 'Booey' Greenwood
Mark Greer
Scott Greer
Elliott Grey
John 'Legs' Griffin
Paul Griffin
Tony Grimes
William Guilfoyle
Terry Hall
Thomas Hall
T F Hallaron
Mary Halstead
Andrew Hampton
Paul Hanrahan
Steve Hanrahan

Bert Hand	J W Irvine	David Latham
Andrew Harrison	David Isaac	John Latham
Stuart D Harrison	Gwyn Jacks	Shaun Lavin
Dave Hart	Joe Jackson	Ben Lawrence
Alan Hartley	Paul Jalofsky	Miles Lawrence
Andrew Hartley	Mark Jenkins	Christopher Lawrenson
Carl Howard Hartley	Michael Jennions	Andy Lea
Clive Hartley	Ronnie Johnson	Lee Anthony Leaf
Fred Hartley	Ben Johnson	Mr Sydney Leatherbarrow
Graeme Hartley	Geoff Johnson	David Lee
Michael Hartley	Lewis Thomas Johnson	Kelvin Letts
Gary Hastie	Michael Johnston	Megan Gabrielle Levick
Chris Hayes	Alun Owen Jones	Jamie Lewis-Bainbridge
Simon Head	Bryn Jones	Stuart Light
Neil Hedley	Darrell Jones	Mark Lightfoot
Doug Heggie	Dave H Jones	Graham Lindsay
Carolyn Heidema	Kevin Jones	Peter Lindsay
Ian R Henderson	Lozzer Jones	Dave Lloyd
Sam Henderson	Maldwyn Owen Jones	Richard Lloyd
Stuart Henderson	Mrs Maxine Jones	Cian Malcolm Loftus
Graham Henshaw	Nerys M Jones	Tony Lord
Joshua Henshaw	Mr Norman D Jones	Ged Lunny
Bernard Hewson	Paul Michael Jones	Barry Lunt
Ben Higham	Richard T Jones	Shaun Lynch
Dale Higham	Robert Jones	Peter Lyons
Zac Higham	Simon Jones	Tommy Lysaght
John Stephanie Holmes	David Thomas Jordan	Thomas James MacDiarmid
Michael Holmes	Edwin Joynson	Bruce Mackenzie
Peter Holmes	Mark Joynson	David Maddox
Jasmine Honey	Dan Kay	Robert S Maguire
Robert John Hoppe	Peter Kay	Robert Mallinson
Austin Horan	Roy Keane	Alan Mansell
Jimmy Horan	Steve Kearney	Tony Marriott
Barry Hornby	Austin Keegan	Roy Marsh
James Hough	James Patrick Keelan	Paul Martin
Stephen Hough	Peter Keelan	Peter Martin
Denis Houghton	Alan Keen	John Mason
Neil Howard	Dean Joseph Kelly	Bill Matthews
Robbie Howard	Robert Kelly	Tommy Matthews
Emma Hughes	Robert Kelly	Wayne Russell Maycock
Gary Hughes	Robert Kennedy	Ken McAlenan
Martin Hughes	Robert F Kennedy	Ben McAllister
Michael Geofrey Hughes	Paul Kennerley	John McAllister
Paul David Hughes	Sean Kennerley	Matthew McAllister
Peter Hughes	Tony Kennils	Paul McAteer
Steven Robert Hughes	Carl Keyes	Jude McCann
Mr Stephen Hughes	Peter Kilkelly	Kevin McCann
William Hughes	Gary King	Les McCann
Kevin Humphreys	Steve Kirk	Linda McCann
L Humphreys	Kevin Knott	Paul McCann
Lorraine Humphreys	Andrew Knowles	Chris McCarten
Peter D Hunt	Perry Lacy	Stephen McCarthy
Ian Hunter	Rob Lacy	Colin McCartney
Christopher Hyams	Adam Lamb	Graeme McConnelly
Jeffrey Wilson Hyland	Bill Landy	Ciaran McConville
John L Inglis	Thomas Langan	Ray McConville

John J McDonald
John S McDonald
Mark McDonald
William McDonald
Sean McDonnell
Jamie McEwan
William McGinnigle
John Wesley McGivern
Steve McGlasson
Alec McGowan
Andy McGreevy
Peter McIlhoney
John McIntyre
Stephen McKee
Graeme McKenna
Chris McKeon
Michael McLaughlin
Steven McLaughlin
Martyn McLean
Mike McLelland
Andrew McLoughlin
David S McMillan
Jimmy G McMillan
Lesley F McMillan
Stephen Malcom McMillan
Paul McQuade
John McQuinn
Anthony Meakin
Ian Mercer
Phil Merricks
Michael Metcalf
Craig Miles
Steven Millar
Amanda Miller
George Miller
George Miller
Michael Miller
Stephen Miller
Colin Milner
Andrew Brian Mitchell
Dave Mitchell
Nick Mitchell
Michael Moan
Andy Molyneux
John Molyneux
Mike Molyneux
Paul Molyneux
Steven Moody
John Moorcroft
Daniel Moore
Joe Moore
Ken Moore (Canada)
David Morecroft
Anthony James Morgan
Gareth Morgan
Gary Morgan

James Morgan
Michael Morgan
Philip Morgan
Phil Morley
Barry Morris
Brian Morrow
Graham Morton
John Stalford Morton
Tom Moss
Michael Mulhaney
Karl Mullen
Neil Mullin
Mum
Peter James Munro
Roger Munsey
Francis Murphy
Loraine Murphy
Michael Murphy
William 'Spud' Murphy
Brian Christopher Murray
Jack Callum Murray
Eric Nall
Brian Navarro
Chris Neil
Edward Neill
Michael Ness
Will Neville
Kevin Nickson
Tony Noone
Christopher Novelli
Matt Novelli
Colin O'Brien
John O'Donnell
Ian O'Grady
Brian O'Rourke
Mariae O'Toole
Al Offlands
Harry Ogden
John Edward Oldham Junior
Andre Otter
Tony Packenham
Roy Park
Barry Parker
Carl Parker
George Parker
Kevin Parkes
Scott Parkins
R J Parkinson
Mr J D Parks
David Parry
John Pattenden
Peter Pattenden
John Philip Pearcey
Chris Pearson
Michael Pearson
Michael H J Peers

Warren Peers
Keith Pegram
Owen Campbell Pemberton
Sandra Pemberton
Sian Penny
Paul Kevin Perry
Aidrian Cornelius 'Pete' Petrie
Aiden Philbin
Brian Phillips
Victor T Phillips
Deborah Physick
Michael Pickles
Carl Pilmore
Fred Pimblett
Gillie Pitcher
Mark Platt
George Plunkett
Laura Poar
Kareen Porschke
David Potter
John Power
Phil Price
Connor Prior
Ian Pritchard
Billy Prophet
Steve Pryce
Anthony Putt
W R Quayle
Brian Quinn
Nikki Quinn
Chris Rafferty
Derek Ralphf
Mr B Rana
Dave Rankin
Thomas Ralph Rathbone
Daniel Rathe
Brian Robert Rattle
W Derek Reading
Rachel Redman
Jack Redrobe
Dave 'Ginger' Rhyl
Steven B Rigby
David Riley
Edward Riley
Luke Riley
Vinny Riley
Paul David Rimmer
Mr Bernard Robb
Clive Roberts
Dewi Roberts
Gary Roberts
Jennifer Roberts
Kenny Roberts
Michala Roberts
Ronald Roberts
Timothy John Roberts

Tomos Huw Roberts
William David Roberts
Jimmy Robinson
Paul D Robinson
Peter Anthony Roche
Arthur Rogers
Colin Rogers
John Rogers
Paul Rogers
David Rolfe
Carl Rollinson
Christy Rooney
Billy Roper
Mark Roscoe
Wayne Roscoe
Michael Routledge
Adam Roxborough
Ron Roxborough
Simon Roxborough
Steve Roxborough
Joseph Rusk
Linda Rusk
Joseph Ryan
Robert Ryan
Alan Stephen Harvey Salisbury
Andre Sambor
Jaqueline Samosa
Richard Samosa
Richie Samosa
George Sargent
Jim Saul
Billy Savage
Ian Savage
Johnny Schunke
Andrew Scott
Gerard Scully
Dr Laurence Seabra
Ron Sigi Seagreaves
Jack Senior
Fred Sephton
Richard Shannon
Peter J Sharpe
Russ Shaw
Albie Sheridan
Tony Shortell
Ian Simpson
Edward Sixsmith
Chris Smith
Dennis Smith
Fred Smith
George J Smith
Keith Smith
Megan Lucy Smith
Peter Edward Smith
Roger David Smith
William John Smith

Simon Smyth
Karl Jon Speakman
Will Speed-Evans
Steven Thomas Stanley
Ian Stevenson
Paul Stewart
Barry Stinchcomb
Thomas Stockton
Michael Stoddart
Jonny Stokkeland
David Stopforth
George Stopforth
Jack Stopforth
James Stowers
Neil Stringfellow
Carl Styles
Stuart Summers
Colin Sumpter
Ian Sumpter
John Sumpter
Kevin Sumpter
Paul Sumpter
Paul Swain
Barney Swift
Kemal Sylvester
Mark-Anthony Tait
Lewis Talbot
Noel Tallent
Christopher D Taylor
Martin Taylor
Tommy Taylor
Tex
Craig Thomas
Ron Thomas
Wayne Thomas
John Thompson
John Thompson
Peter A Thompson
Tracey Thompson
Hugo Thurman
Lee Thwaite
Nick Tinsley
Edwin Tomlinson
Tommy
Liam Toolan
Phillip Daniel Torres
Stephen Traynor
Stephen Traynor
Eddie Treble
Liam Truman
John Valente
Mr C Van Breemen
Alan Waddington
Tracy Waddington
Stephen Wainwright
Aaron 'Azza' Walker

Allan Walker
George Walker
Karen Walker
Kevin Walker
Kyle Walker
Susan Walker
Brian Wall
Paul Steven Walmsley
Bob Walsh
David Ward
Jade Ward
Lee Ward
Phillippe Washington-Jones
Ian Watkinson
Andrew Watson
Jimmy Watts
Frank Webster
Paul Webster
Robert Webster
Ian West
Donny Wevill
Alfred Thomas White
John White
Michael Paul White
Bill Whorton
Liam Wignall
Marc Wilding
Paul Wildridge
Billy Wilkes
Dave Wilkes
Neil Wilkes
William T Wilkinson
Andy A J Williams
Carl Williams
Colin Paul Williams
Daniel John Williams
Gordon A E Williams
Martin Charles Williams
Samuel J Williams
Bob Wilson
Stan Wilson
Stephen Wiseman
Karl Wong
Liam Wong
Barry Wood
Mr Robert Woods
Roger Woods
Mike Woolrich
Mark Woosey
Martin Lee Woosey
Neill Woosey
Joe Wright
Ian Wylie
Gaynor Wynne
Graham Yates
Jordan Young
Wesley Young

SPORT MEDIA
Trinity Mirror North West

Acknowledgements

A lot of time, effort and hard work has gone into compiling this book from, not just myself, but a wide range of people. I must start by thanking everyone who took the time to put their memories into words or write articles for me or allowed me to reproduce articles that they had previously written. I'm also grateful to everyone who made time available for me to interview them - too many to mention individually - and to my colleagues Ken Rogers, Alan Jewell, Gavin Kirk and Ric George who contributed key articles.

My thanks also go to Paul Dove and Dan Willoughby for all their hard work on the production side of things, Barry Parker for access to his vast array of memorabilia and the staff at the Liverpool Daily Post and Echo library who have been inundated with requests for photos. I must also give a huge thank you to Liverpool FC's museum curator, Stephen Done, who not only provided a wealth of valuable information but also gave us access to some of the unusual and spectacular photography contained within the book, some of which was taken by Len Humphries.

Adrian Killen and Tom Preston also deserve honourable mentions for their work and research into Liverpool's history which has proved useful for me, as does Gary Morgan for providing me with photos of the Kop during its rebuilding.

Other articles and recollections have been reproduced after first appearing elsewhere. The memories from Phil Thompson, David Moores, Joey Jones, Peter Thompson, Nigel Clough, John Osborne and Nigel Martyn are taken from various editions of the Liverpool Echo. Other stories from Joe Fagan, David Moores, Roy Evans, Ray Clemence, Ron Yeats, Steve Heighway and Paul Jones have been reproduced from various Liverpool FC official matchday programmes and 'LFC Magazine'. The pieces from The Independent and 90 Minutes, and the excellent cartoon, were originally published in 1994 and 1999 respectively. The tales told by Rogan Taylor, Mike McCartney and Stuart Hall were taken from 'The Last Night of the Kop' tribute programme, compiled by Intermedia PR in 1994 while Nessie Shankly's words first appeared in the Liverpool Daily Post and Gordon West's recollections have been reproduced from 'The Evertonian'. I'm also indebted to every Kopite who responded to our adverts in The Kop magazine or on www.icliverpool.co.uk and took the time to contribute their stories. It was impossible to include them all but thanks to everyone of you for all your efforts. We have done our best to research the copyright of every image and acknowledge those we may have missed. Finally, thanks to my girlfriend Leila for all her support.

Chris McLoughlin